WORLD BEAT

International

Poetry now

WORLD BEAT

FROM
NEW DIRECTIONS

EDITED BY ELIOT WEINBERGER

A NEW DIRECTIONS BOOK

Publisher's Note: The poems in this anthology are collected from books either published by New Directions or soon to be published by New Directions, and are copyrighted as follows, in order of appearance: Octavio Paz, "Response and Reconciliation" © 2006 by Marie José Paz, Heir of Octavio Paz, and translation © 2006 by Eliot Weinberger; Luljeta Lleshanaku, *Fresco* © 2002 by Luljeta Lleshanaku, and translation © 2002 by Henry Israeli, Ukzenel Buçpapa, Shpresa Qatipi, & Qazim Sheme; Dunya Mikhail, *The War Works Hard* © 2005 by Dunya Mikhail, and translation © 2005 by Elizabeth Winslow; Forrest Gander, *Eye Against Eye* © 2005 by Forrest Gander; Gu Cheng, *Sea of Dreams* © 1993 by Gu Cheng, © 1993 by Huayi Publishing House, and translation © 2005 by Joseph R. Allen; Anne Carson, *Glass, Irony and God* © 1995 by Anne Carson; Bei Dao, *Unlock* © 2000 by Zhao Zhenkai, translation © 2000 by Eliot Weinberger & Iona Man-Cheong, "Ramallah" and "The Rose of Time" © 2006 by Zhao Zhenkai, and translation © Eliot Weinberger & Zhao Zhenkai; Nathaniel Mackey, *Splay Anthem* © 2006 by Nathaniel Mackey; Michael Palmer, *At Passages* © 1995 by Michael Palmer, *The Lion Bridge: Selected Poems 1972-1995* © 1998 by Michael Palmer, *The Promises of Glass* © 2000 by Michael Palmer, *The Company of Moths* © 2005 by Michael Palmer; Homero Aridjis, *Eyes to See Otherwise* © 2001 by Homero Aridjis, and translation © 2001 by George McWhirter; Aharon Shabtai, *J'Accuse* © 2002 by Aharon Shabtai, translation © 2003 by Peter Cole, "Hebrew Culture," "Hope," and "Sharon Resembles a Person" © 2006 by Aharon Shabtai, and translation © 2006 by Peter Cole; Susan Howe, *The Nonconformist's Memorial* © 1993 by Susan Howe; Inger Christensen, *alphabet* © 1981, 2000 by Inger Christensen, and translation © 2000 by Susanna Nied; Gustaf Sobin, *Breath's Burial* © 1995 by Gustaf Sobin; Rosmarie Waldrop, *Blindsight* © 2003 by Rosmarie Waldrop; Gennady Aygi, *Child-And-Rose* © 2002 by Gennady Aygi, and translation © 2003 by Peter France; Hans Faverey, *Against the Forgetting* © 1994, 2004 by Lela Zecković-Faverey, and translation © 1994, 2004 by Francis R. Jones; Jerome Rothenberg, *A Paradise of Poets* © 1999 by Jerome Rothenberg; Kazuko Shiraishi, *Let Those Who Appear* © 2002 by Kazuko Shiraishi, and translation © 2002 by Samuel Grolmes & Yumiko Tsumura; Tomas Tranströmer, "The Great Enigma" © 2006 by Tomas Tranströmer, and translation © 2006 by Robin Fulton, published by arrangement with Bloodaxe Books; Kamau Brathwaite, *Middle Passages* © 1992, 1993 by Kamau Brathwaite; Charles Tomlinson, *Selected Poems* © 1997 by Charles Tomlinson; Nicanor Parra, *Antipoems: How to Look Better and Feel Great* © 2004 by Nicanor Parra, and translation © 2004 by Liz Werner.

Manufactured in the United States of America
New Directions Books are printed on acid-free paper
First published as New Directions Paperbook 1034 in 2006
Published simultaneously in Canada by Penguin Books Canada Limited

Library of Congress Cataloging-in-Publication Data
World beat : international poetry now from New Directions / edited by Eliot Weinberger.
    p. cm.
  ISBN-13: 978-0-8112-1651-7 (alk. paper)
  ISBN-10: 0-8112-1651-9 (alk. paper)
 1. Poetry—20th century—Translations into English. 2. English poetry—20th century.
 3. American poetry—20th century. I. Weinberger, Eliot.
  PN6101.W49   2006
  808.81'04—dc22

                                                    2005035049

New Directions Books are published for James Laughlin
by New Directions Publishing Corporation
80 Eighth Avenue, New York, NY 10011

CONTENTS

Preface   vii

Octavio Paz
    translated from the Spanish by Eliot Weinberger   1

Luljeta Lleshanaku
    translated from the Albanian by Henry Israeli & others   6

Dunya Mikhail
    translated from the Arabic by Elizabeth Winslow   14

Forrest Gander   25

Gu Cheng
    translated from the Chinese by Joseph R. Allen   35

Anne Carson   46

Bei Dao
    translated from the Chinese by Eliot Weinberger
    & Iona Man-Cheong   59

Nathaniel Mackey   70

Michael Palmer   83

Homero Aridjis
    translated from the Spanish by George McWhirter   95

Aharon Shabtai
    translated from the Hebrew by Peter Cole   103

Susan Howe   114

INGER CHRISTENSEN
    translated from the Danish by Susanna Nied   123

GUSTAF SOBIN   137

ROSMARIE WALDROP   147

GENNADY AYGI
    translated from the Russian by Peter France   159

HANS FAVEREY
    translated from the Dutch by Francis R. Jones   169

JEROME ROTHENBERG   179

KAZUKO SHIRAISHI
    translated from the Japanese by Samuel Grolmes
    & Yumiko Tsumura   185

TOMAS TRANSTRÖMER
    translated from the Swedish by Robin Fulton   191

KAMAU BRATHWAITE   203

CHARLES TOMLINSON   218

ROBERT CREELEY   226

NICANOR PARRA
    translated from the Spanish by Liz Werner   236

Contributors   243
Index   255

Since its founding in 1936 by James Laughlin, New Directions has been the primary American publisher of international poetry. It was the first, or among the earliest, to present translations of Apollinaire, Bobrowski, Brecht, Breton, Cendrars, Char, Cocteau, Eluard, García Lorca, Huidobro, Jacob, Jarry, Lautréamont, Mayakovsky, Michaux, Montale, Neruda, Pasternak, Paz, Reverdy, Rilke, Seferis, Supervielle, Ungaretti, Vallejo, and Valéry, among many others, and for decades it had the only available editions of Baudelaire and Rimbaud. These were poets intended to be read in the New Directions context of its American vanguard: Pound, Williams, H.D., Oppen, Reznikoff, Rexroth, Patchen, Rukeyser, Merton, Olson, Duncan, Snyder, Ferlinghetti, Levertov, among them.

This tradition of the new and this global perspective continue, yet where there were once a few hundred poetry books published each year in the U.S., there are now many thousands. Where once unknown poets were put on the map merely by being published by New Directions, they are now often lost in the mountains of printed matter.

The purpose of this anthology, then, is simple. Here are selections from most of the foreign poets, known and little-known, published in recent years by New Directions, alongside some of the Americans. It is an anthology that, unlike most, may be easily read cover to cover; a collection of poems that, one hopes, illuminate and delight; an introduction to the individual poets, which may lead readers to their books; and a brief outline of some of the things that are happening in world poetry now. Because of the inevitable time-lag in translation, "now" is defined as work written or published in the last twenty years. The "world" here includes the United States. Contrary to the usual anthology practice of "them or us," it is a reading of these Americans as international literature.

The book opens with the last poem of Octavio Paz, previously unpublished in book form. Paz is a typical New Directions story:

The first translation of his poems, anywhere in the world, appeared in a ND anthology in 1946; Paz often later remarked that he took this as the first sign that what he was writing was of interest outside of Mexico. (And John Ashbery has said that discovering those poems as a teenager was his first revelation of modern poetry.) Paz here marks a transition from the old to the new New Directions, from the modern classics to what, quite probably, will be future classics. After Paz, the anthology proceeds according to chronological birth order of the poets, from the youngest to the oldest. It includes two poets who died young, Gu Cheng and Hans Faverey, and, sadly, two poets who died as this book was being edited, Robert Creeley and Gustaf Sobin. It ends, completing the circle, with recent poems from Nicanor Parra, who was born the same year as Paz. Some of the poets are partially represented with work written or translated since their last New Directions book.

All translation sends the essential message that one's own culture is not enough, and that the way to avoid intellectual stagnation is to learn from other ways of thinking about, perceiving, luxuriating and despairing in, the world. This book appears at a moment when the United States is particularly self-absorbed. Less than a fifth of its citizens have passports; a third of its high school students cannot find the Pacific Ocean on a world map; its rulers dream without embarrassment of a global empire. Poetry, though not the salvation of the world, presents a small alternate model: an endless net of individual dialogues between writers, and between writers and readers, regardless of governments, nations, and communal identities. Its books are a way out of one's world and a way into the world at large.

ELIOT WEINBERGER

WORLD BEAT

Octavio Paz

translated from the Spanish by Eliot Weinberger

Response and Reconciliation

I.

Ah life! Does no one answer?
His words rolled, bolts of lightning etched
in years that were boulders and now are mist.
Life never answers.
It has no ears and doesn't hear us;
it doesn't speak, it has no tongue.
It neither goes nor stays:
we are the ones who speak,
the ones who go,
while we hear from echo to echo, year to year,
our words rolling through a tunnel with no end.

That which we call life
hears itself within us, speaks with our tongues,
and through us, knows itself.
As we portray it, we become its mirror, we invent it.
An invention of an invention: it creates us
without knowing what it has created,
we are an accident that thinks.
It is a creature of reflections
we create by thinking,
and it hurls into fictitious abysses.
The depths, the transparencies
where it floats or sinks: not life, its idea.
It is always on the other side and is always other,
has a thousand bodies and none,
never moves and never stops,
it is born to die, and is born at death.

Is life immortal? Don't ask life,
for it doesn't even know what life is.
We are the ones who know
that one day it too must die and return
to the beginning, the inertia of the origin.
The end of yesterday, today, and tomorrow,
the dissipation of time
and of nothing, its opposite.
Then—will there be a then?
will the primigenius spark light
the matrix of the worlds,
a perpetual re-beginning of a senseless whirling?
No one answers, no one knows.
We only know that to live is to live for.

II.

Sudden spring, a girl who wakes
on a green bed guarded by thorns;
tree of noon, heavy with oranges:
your tiny suns, fruits of cool fire,
summer gathers them in transparent baskets;
the fall is severe, its cold light
sharpens its knife against the red maples;
Januaries and Februaries: their beards are ice,
and their eyes sapphires that April liquefies;
the wave that rises, the wave that stretches out,
appearances-disappearances
on the circular road of the year.

All that we see, all that we forget,
the harp of the rain, the inscription of the lightning,
the hurried thoughts, reflections turned to birds,
the doubts of the path as it meanders,
the wailing of the wind

as it carves the faces of the mountains,
the moon on tiptoe over the lake,
the breezes in gardens, the throbbing of night,
the camps of stars on the burnt field,
the battle of reflections on the white salt flats,
the fountain and its monologue,
the held breath of outstretched night
and the river that entwines it, the pine under the evening star
and the waves, instant statues, on the sea,
the flock of clouds that the wind herds
through drowsy valleys, the peaks, the chasms,
time turned to rock, frozen eras,
time maker of roses and plutonium,
time that makes as it razes.

The ant, the elephant, the spider, and the sheep,
our strange world of terrestrial creatures
that are born, eat, kill, sleep, play, couple,
and somehow know that they die;
our world of humanity, far and near,
the animal with eyes in its hands
that tunnels through the past and examines the future,
with its histories and uncertainties,
the ecstasy of the saint, the sophisms of the evil,
the elation of lovers, their meetings, their contentions,
the insomnia of the old man counting his mistakes,
the criminal and the just: a double enigma,
the Father of the People, his crematory parks,
his forests of gallows and obelisks of skulls,
the victorious and the defeated,
the long sufferings and the one happy moment,
the builder of houses and the one who destroys them,
this paper where I write, letter by letter,
which you glance at with distracted eyes,
all of them and all of it, all
is the work of time that begins and ends.

III.

From birth to death time surrounds us
with its intangible walls.
We fall with the centuries, the years, the minutes.
Is time only a falling, only a wall?
For a moment, sometimes, we see
—not with our eyes but with our thoughts—
time resting in a pause.
The world half-opens and we glimpse
the immaculate kingdom,
the pure forms, presences
unmoving, floating
on the hour, a river stopped:
truth, beauty, numbers, ideas
—and goodness, a word buried
in our century.
                    A moment without weight or duration,
a moment outside the moment:
thought sees, our eyes think.

Triangles, cubes, the sphere, the pyramid
and the other geometrical figures
thought and drawn by mortal eyes
but which have been here since the beginning,
are, still legible, the world, its secret writing,
the reason and the origin of the turning of things,
the axis of the changes, the unsupported pivot
that rests on itself, a reality without a shadow.
The poem, the piece of music, the theorem,
unpolluted presences born from the void,
are delicate structures
built over an abyss:
infinities fit into their finite forms,
and chaos too is ruled by their hidden symmetry.

Because we know it, we are not an accident:
chance, redeemed, returns to order.
Tied to the earth and to time,
a light and weightless ether,
thought supports the worlds and their weight,
whirlwinds of suns turned
into a handful of signs
on a random piece of paper.
Wheeling swarms
of transparent evidence
where the eyes of understanding
drink a water simple as water.
The universe rhymes with itself,
it unfolds and is two and is many
without ceasing to be one.
Motion, a river that runs endlessly
with open eyes through the countries of vertigo
—there is no above nor below, what is near is far—
returns to itself
                    —without returning, now turned
into a fountain of stillness.
Tree of blood, man feels, thinks, flowers,
and bears strange fruits: words.
What is thought and what is felt entwine,
we touch ideas: they are bodies and they are numbers.

And while I say what I say
time and space fall dizzyingly,
restlessly. They fall in themselves.
Man and the galaxy return to silence.
Does it matter? Yes—but it doesn't matter:
we know that silence is music and that
we are a chord in this concert.

LULJETA LLESHANAKU

translated from the Albanian by HENRY ISRAELI & OTHERS

Half Past Three

Half past three. The hour when all matter
separates into cause and effect.
My bed floats in the shallow waters of a lagoon
its legs cast in bronze
gripping the carpet.

An ax strikes rhythmically
against the sequoia trunk
of world harmony.
The same old history
no winners or losers . . .

The beginning and the end, both cryptic and vague:
two midwives pushing cruelly at my belly. Nearby,
like a burnt-out log
a cat, bored of being stroked,
dozes on its paws.

Half past three in the morning, my elements break down
into air, water, fire, earth,
until I am unrecognizable.

I am not my own enemy. My enemy is the light.
And the Yellow River of China.
With the tragic history
of bridges arching over it.

Still Life

Here in a summer full of dust
the dampness of winter
trails us into dark corners.

I bought the shoes days ago
but they remain untouched in the box
heel to heel.

Blessed is the sunbeam that falls upon us
like the eye of a stranger focused on a *natura morte*.
A platter of the season's finest fruit
so plump, and nestled among it, a shiny dagger.
It's not dangerous
but as alluring and peaceful
as the fruit that surrounds it.

What has become of us?
My hands, skillful and transparent,
slice the atmosphere into rabbit feed.

Another new pair of shoes
to help you enjoy a stroll around the grounds.
Since you've left I dream of only one thing:
the sound they would make
in the evening
as you reach the front door.

Electrolytes

For a long time now
your kisses have burned me
and your clean body frightened me
like sheets in a surgery ward
and your breath disappearing in my lungs
is like lilies dropped into a cesspool
in the dead of winter.

For a long time now
I have felt ashamed of my freedom.
Every day I pull a stake off your fence
and burn it for warmth.

My freedom . . . your freedom . . .
An atmosphere alive with electricity
my soul pawned for a nickel
yours slowly deserted by its ions
and growing smaller every day.

Absence

The moon
nicotine of a kiss . . .

A sideways glance
like the mast of a pirate ship
beyond a distant island.

Betrayed

Betrayed woman, like an outgrown shirt
like the worn hole on an old belt
like a starched collar . . .
Betrayed woman, who wakes from nightmares
feeling like dirt in the corner of an eye
like a kettle taken off the stove
still steaming.

Her hips sway rhythmically
in a chewing motion
as she moves diagonally through the house.
The children, oh the children, bubbling forth!
Late at night, an aluminum lid
above a sprig of parsley—
limp nerve floating in a cold lemony broth.

There is a betrayed man, too,
betrayed by dark angels
with shoulders covered in ferns.

Betrayed men and women
accept fate nobly
as one would accept a murky glass of water
at a rest stop along the way.
Betrayed men and women
on a long journey.

Chronic Appendicitis

How odd this winter is.
A felled tree in a forest
hallucinates skeletons
dragged out of the body.

Wet kisses on a bed of wet leaves
the shudder of a notary's hand
curving symmetrically against a sky
covered in paper and glue.

The inner light of things would be enough
to fuel our chlorophyll
for we are as free as germs . . .
we are frail trees, gracious plants,
half our bodies
bent in the wind.

The exhalation of cars in traffic
the exhalation of a dying February:
carbon dioxide creaking forth from lungs
like bedsprings in an orphanage.

February's edict slowly expires
and again rain, rain, and more rain—
rain moaning under the excruciating suffering
of chronic appendicitis
rain without thunder, without lightning.

The Awakening of the Eremite

All ideas escape me
one by one, secretly slipping away
like witnesses to a political crime.

When they crawl back, tortoise-slow
the air trembles nervously in its wheelchair
and I rise.

My shadow, liberated, wanders
the room on an invisible cord
gravity sudden as a dead fly
dropped from a spider's nest.

All ideas escape me—
how far this time I cannot say.
Perhaps they'll turn up in a train station somewhere
in a town where they are unwelcome.

Outside, the moon presses against the hills
like a prophet's tongue against his palate.

The walls, protesting,
return my voice two, three, four times over
an echo horribly replicating itself
while slowly inside me
the eremite awakens.

Out of Boredom

Out of boredom
roebucks lie down with toads
night swallows the moon
like a sleeping pill
and sky becomes lace
on the veil of a dreamer.
A white strand of smoke rises
like a cypress
from a burning cigarette.

The clock tower warbles a soldier's old tune
the one he whistles as he polishes his steel crutches.
An old woman's fingers, anxious as a child's
held out for a nickel, tap a tarot card.

Out of boredom
footsteps consume the streets
with the hunger of Chaplin in a silent film.
Out of boredom the soul, like an amoeba,
expands and divides
so that it will no longer be alone.

Self-Defense

Confined
to a tent of soldiers
who will never return home.
If you try to leave
you will step on the bodies
sleeping beside you.

You have nowhere to go.
The stars
those witches' fingernails
stir your destiny through the fog.

In the corner
among ashes
you count the holes in your old blanket.
You breathe in bits of everyone's dreams.
Like an iceberg you ignore all borders.

While in your blood
surprisingly enough
the leukocytes multiply.

DUNYA MIKHAIL
translated from the Arabic by ELIZABETH WINSLOW

The War Works Hard

How magnificent the war is!
How eager
and efficient!
Early in the morning,
it wakes up the sirens
and dispatches ambulances
to various places,
swings corpses through the air,
rolls stretchers to the wounded,
summons rain
from the eyes of mothers,
digs into the earth
dislodging many things
from under the ruins . . .
Some are lifeless and glistening,
others are pale and still throbbing . . .
It produces the most questions
in the minds of children,
entertains the gods
by shooting fireworks and missiles
into the sky,
sows mines in the fields
and reaps punctures and blisters,
urges families to emigrate,
stands beside the clergymen
as they curse the devil
(poor devil, he remains
with one hand in the searing fire) . . .
The war continues working, day and night.
It inspires tyrants

to deliver long speeches,
awards medals to generals
and themes to poets.
It contributes to the industry
of artificial limbs,
provides food for flies,
adds pages to the history books,
achieves equality
between killer and killed,
teaches lovers to write letters,
accustoms young women to waiting,
fills the newspapers
with articles and pictures,
builds new houses
for the orphans,
invigorates the coffin makers,
gives grave diggers
a pat on the back
and paints a smile on the leader's face.
The war works with unparalleled diligence!
Yet no one gives it
a word of praise.

An Urgent Call

This is an urgent call
for the American soldier Lynndie
to immediately return to her homeland.
She suffers from a dangerous virus
in her heart.
She is pregnant
and is sinking in deep mud.
She sinks deeper and deeper
as she hears: "Good job!"

Hurry up, Lynndie,
go back to America now.
Don't worry,
you will not lose your job.
There are prisons everywhere,
prisons with big black holes,
and great shivering,
and consecutive flashes,
and tremblings that convey messages
with no language
in a blind galaxy.
Don't worry,
nobody will force you
to feed the birds
when you carry a gun.
Nobody will force you
to work for the environment
when you wear combat boots.
Don't worry,
we will send an email to God
to tell Him
that the barbarians
were the solution.
Don't worry.
Take a sick leave
and release your baby
from your body,
but don't forget
to hide those terrible pictures,
the pictures of you dancing in the mud.
Keep them away
from his or her eyes.
Hide them, please.
You don't want your child to cry out:
The prisoners are naked . . .

America

Please don't ask me, America.
I don't remember
on which street,
with whom,
or under which star.
Don't ask me . . .
I don't remember
the colors of the people
or their signatures.
I don't remember if they had
our faces
and our dreams,
if they were singing
or not,
writing from the left
or the right
or not writing at all,
sleeping in houses
on sidewalks
or in airports,
making love or not making love.
Please don't ask me, America.
I don't remember their names
or their birthplaces.
People are grass—
they grow everywhere, America.
Don't ask me . . .
I don't remember
what time it was,
what the weather was like,
which language,
or which flag.
Don't ask me . . .

I don't remember
how long they walked under the sun
or how many died.
I don't remember
the shapes of the boats
or the number of stops . . .
How many suitcases they carried
or left behind,
if they came complaining
or without complaint.
Stop your questioning, America,
and offer your hand
to the tired
on the other shore.
Offer it without questions
or waiting lists.
What good is it to gain the whole world
if you lose your soul, America?
Who said that the sky
would lose all of its stars
if night passed without answers?
America, leave your questionnaires to the river
and leave me to my lover.
It has been a long time,
we are two distant, rippling shores
and the river wriggles between us
like a well-cooked fish.
It has been a long time, America,
(longer than the stories of my grandmother
in the evening)
and we are waiting for the signal
to throw our shell in the river.
We know that the river is full
of shells
this last one

wouldn't matter,
yet it matters to the shell . . .
Why do you ask all these questions?
You want our fingerprints
in all languages
and I have become old,
older than my father.
He used to tell me in the evenings
when no trains ran:
One day, we will go to America.
One day, we will go
and sing a song,
translated or not translated,
at the Statue of Liberty.
And now, America, now
I come to you without my father.
The dead ripen faster
than Indian figs,
but they never grow older, America.
They come in shifts of shadow and light
in our dreams
and as shooting stars
or curve in rainbows
over the houses we left behind.
They sometimes get angry
if we keep them waiting long . . .
What time is it now?
I am afraid I will receive
your registered mail, America,
in this hour
which is good for nothing . . .
So I will toy with the freedom
like teasing a pet cat.
I wouldn't know what else
to do with it

in this hour
which is good for nothing . . .
And my sweetheart
there, on the opposite
shore of the river
carries a flower for me.
And I—as you know—
dislike faded flowers.
I do like my sweetheart's handwriting
shining each day in the mail.
I salvage it from among ad fliers
and a special offer:
"Buy One Get One Free"
and an urgent promotional announcement:
"Win a million dollars
if you subscribe to this magazine!"
and bills to be paid
in monthly installments.
I like my sweetheart's handwriting,
though it gets shakier every day.
We have a single picture
just one picture, America.
I want it.
I want that moment
(forever out of reach)
in the picture which I know
from every angle:
the circular moment of sky.
Imagine, America,
if one of us drops out of the picture
and leaves the album full
of loneliness,
or if life becomes
a camera
without film.

Imagine, America!
Without a frame,
the night will take us
tomorrow,
darling,
tomorrow
the night
will take us
without a frame.
We will shake the museums
forever from their sleep,
fix our broken clocks
so we'll tick in the public squares
whenever the train
passes us by.
Tomorrow,
darling,
tomorrow
we will bloom:
two leaves of a tree
we will try not to be
too graceful and green
and in time
we will tumble down like dancers
taken by the wind
to the places whose names
we'll have forgotten.
We will be glad for the sake of turtles
because they persist along their way . . .
Tomorrow,
darling,
tomorrow
I'll look at your eyes
to see your new wrinkles,
the lines of our future dreams.

As you braid my gray hair
under rain
or sun
or moon,
every hair will know
that nothing happens
twice,
every kiss a country
with a history
a geography
and a language
with joy and sadness
with war
and ruins
and holidays
and ticking clocks . . .
And when the pain in your neck returns, darling,
you will not have time to complain
and won't be concerned.
The pain will remain inside us
coy as snow that won't melt.
Tomorrow, darling,
tomorrow
two rings will jingle
in the wooden box.
They have been shining for a long time
on two trembling hands,
entangled
by the absence.
Tomorrow,
the whiteness will expose
all its colors
as we celebrate the return
of what was lost
or concealed

in the whiteness.
How should I know, America,
which of the colors
was the most joyful
tumultuous
alienated
or assimilated
of them all?
How would I know, America?

Non-Military Statements

1
Yes, I did write in my letter
that I would wait for you forever.
I didn't mean exactly "forever,"
I just included it for the rhythm.

2
No, he was not among them.
There were so many of them!
More than I've seen in my life
on any television screen.
And yet he was not among them.

3
It has no carvings
or arms.
It always remains there
in front of the television
this empty chair.

4

I dream of a magic wand
that changes my kisses to stars.
At night you can gaze at them
and know they are innumerable.

5

I thank everyone I don't love.
They don't cause me heartache;
they don't make me write long letters;
they don't disturb my dreams.
I don't wait for them anxiously;
I don't read their horoscopes in magazines;
I don't dial their numbers;
I don't think of them.
I thank them a lot.
They don't turn my life upside down.

6

I drew a door
to sit behind, ready
to open the door
as soon as you arrive.

Forrest Gander

Mission Thief

Picking up toward evening
       bay breezes quicken
       the Mission and
       fuchsia petals plop
       onto slabs of root-tilted sidewalk
       a local tectonics we maneuver
       you and I fecund with our
       renewed vows en route
       to La Cumbre with its Aztec
       mural and gorditos
       at the curb, windows opaque,
       a black '75 Cadillac
       rocks high up and drops
       back on pneumatic shocks
       a whiff of carne asada
       poles mummified with posters:
       Has Visto Este Niño / Thrash Polka at Slims—
while

                        five blocks away
      the imminent lays its egg
      in the eye of evening and
      what begins as tenderness
      will end at Calvary
      for whose devotion can I claim
      to aim wholly at you if holding
      your hand even so
      my eyes swivel
      to see the figure at the door

with dim desire or is it
nostalgia finally, mere registration,
an animal impulse
tightens the plexus—
only at the crossing only
through horizons—
three blocks away
a white-haired man
the collar of his jacket
stained with sweat
closes his saddlebags and leans
his bicycle, all he owns,
against the pharmacy wall
while a panhandler puts down
his bagged bottle
by the lightpost and watches

you reach for
            my hand as we cross Dolores I spit
            sidewise into my shadow
            when you aren't looking
            the monitor on a stool outside the Mission Revival
            plays a live feed
            of the sermon within
            a bleak scene few men
            one child about twelve
            sweaty preacher's sthenic rant
            dressed well
            a parishioner slips out
            through front doors but before
            they close, another—one
            of us, the assembly of voyeurs—
            ushers herself in:
            so water evaporating from treetops

siphons water through leaf
which siphons water
through xylem up the trunk
from roots maybe when
one escapes
another is sucked inside
who will rescue her?
not me and not open-mouthed
opportunity
eyeing the bike against the wall

                                    we do not see
the man the panhandler steal the bike
though others can
two sparrows titter in fescue
on the traffic island
we continue to stroll
in urban intimacy the same
tuned rhythm our synced steps
mark us a couple
a couplet on the page of scrawled noise
men sawing pavement at the corner
thick rap bass thumping
from open cars a Harley
growls around Guerrero
Mexican songs at the café we pass
a splash of Mandarin washes over
the protected pool of our taking-it-in
only at the crossing only through horizons
with roses for sale, approaching the pair
eating at a curbside table,
an ink-haired Guatemalan girl in a red dress
her shyness hovers at the edge of their plates like a fly
the bicycle thief wobbles our way

long strips of stratus make it
           a dropjaw sunset I stumble and
           from behind you
           catch the swing phase of your walk
           erotic your left foot pigeon-toed
           hips narrow as a boy's
           but what hatched in the alley and left
           that urine stink and sparrows
           thikke as motes in the sonne-beem
           and two starlings
           their wings scissored behind them
           like mournful rabbis
           I used to imagine strangers naked
           you say now I imagine them in coffins
           the back of our hands touch
           you squeeze my thumb the body
           ambiguously subject and
           object a dog tied to a fireplug sneezes
           the man passing by says Bless you
           a little sordid and still warm leftover
           flan-yellow of day remains
           before what was once called civil-dark
           when it grew too dim to work and
           the ice man with his iron-scorpion
           dragged to a kitchen his last block
           already the future is cued up and closing in
           summoning us to what?
           the thief peddles toward us
           though we have not seen him

                              when you turn
           your face to ask me if
           Mexicans call hummingbirds colibrí
           or chupaflor flower-sucker the light

reveals your irises' steel rims
dark hoops that hold the blue in
and do we invent this privacy
the privilege to brim with each other
as though our rillet might be
deducted from the mainstream
as if we were stirred together
past mere propinquity
and the desperate and enraged
were eased by such a day
as in that story of the wolf
unstalking its prey the familiar
rapture I presume you feel
with me even as I tongue
the prickles in my throat
that foretell a cold and step back
to the brink

of thee, smudged
newspaper print where your
fingers brushed your nose
at once we sense commotion ahead
as faces one by one like cards
when a bet is called
flip their open expression
toward us
what is happening
hurtles our way in shouts shouts
as if something were
being birthed, alert
I see the man on bicycle
under a neon taqueria sign—
only at the crossing only through
horizons between—someone yells
something inarticulate
almost to us

                              he is racing
          recklessly up the sidewalk—startled
          pedestrians jump aside—
          already plummeting
          from prospective to present
          his counterpoint
          divorcing you from me
          from the rhythm of our tangency
          our breaking into *my* and *my*
          I lurch and cannot feel yet and fail to rise
          into the revision
          of circumstance as though
          I tumbled from stairs
          to a spot-lit stage where you were
          cut off from me by the light
          a sidewalk of strangers
          severed from concerns that seconds prior
          perfectly contained them
          waylaid and yielding their leads
          for the role of audience
          the drama hurrying on its way
          the head of event expanding
          the dark head of event crowning before us

and it still is not clear
          what is happening what
          is impinging on us
          an obligation I hear
          an indecipherable whinny of alarm
          the immediate stamping in its stall
          as the thief nears our end of the block
          as light that left a galaxy
          in the Hercules cluster
          600 million years ago

now burns through the horizon
and ignites a life
that was never beyond my seeing
and the same wakes up from itself
pain of the eye overwhelmed by light
while I strain for clues
in the surprised faces
the many misconstrued bodies
off balance on pause
to isolate the bicyclist
in his singular tumult
he who supplants you
who makes his claim
greater on me
he himself custodian now
of this present in which
against inertia I strain to act
but

                    how quickly he penetrates
the blister of my regard
from which you've been extracted
as the world goes quiet
and the event of identification
gathers me into its theme
handlebar and rear-rack panniers
swinging side to side half
standing on pedals whose
wild joggling wide-wet eyes urge
No no don't stop me
I mean to grab for his arm
but your hand stays mine and
from an infinite distance
I recall you

your presence
blows in, a red petal,
three of us
briefly enjoined
pooling our volitions
you tug my shirt
my hand slaps his neck
half-assed scuffle my
knuckles scrape the stucco wall

as he flails
at me I hear but
whom do I hear?
my failure all along to
secern even you
who are saying *No*
the word rings and through the ring
a thin scarf of disapproval
draws across my vague intent
awkward in the struggle
to hold him to judge what
effort to make with whom
am I thrashing
a bent stalk a question mark
for a backbone
my hand touching his shoulder
so tentative and slow
the gesture might be taken
for an act of deputation
a surplus of devotion the
bestowal of meaning then
he stiff-arms me and
I turn

                                    like the other
           spectators, a pure stare
           now a singularity uncoupled once again
           that readily from you like the dissolving glow
           of a clicked-off light
           the floater behind a closed eye
           and so combined elements
           on the stalk of an instant
           unpetal their parts in wind
           a hand bleeding a man on bicycle
           a murky sense of restraint which is you
           breached from the *we* I presupposed
           lifted from the felt
           background and placed here again
           near but across the caesura
           the rent stanza in our accord
           as what I am cracks
           into two acts
           and one replays the scene
           revising it toward

some imagined salvific end
           if trajectory
           is divisible
           I gauge the thief's increasing
           distance from me
           instinctively as when flying
           I measure the gap
           from jet to ground
           with an image of my body falling
           a red petal
           he veers to the street
           and something summons me again
           a wheeze spins me around

to see a white-haired man
in a sluggish run
slather of mucus under
pigeon-hole nostrils, his gaze
nailed ahead *at the crossing*
my eyes put on his face
his mouth a gasping rictus
as he plods past
never to catch
what

                  lulled on routine and self
and casual neglect I let slip
rooted in place around me
a block of storefronts and trees
a man on foot falling farther behind
the one on bike
the rest of us unrescued
stopped in time transfixed
to this stark spectacle of our separateness
making its stand
hammering its horizons home
behind which each of us says I don't know
who you are
you never broke through me
the key makes no sound
when you go to play
the world shifts
along a hairline crack
you can't tell
what is happening
until it moves on and is gone
as someone and someone's grief
careen around a corner

GU CHENG

translated from the Chinese by JOSEPH R. ALLEN

The Holy Child Descends

I go out
in search of a bathroom
and see time there, unconscious time
serving well, with its clicking sounds
walking about dressed in white
a monster gnashing its teeth

Life is imprinted on the floor
and there are also stations and a driving staff
lawns in large swaths
maize, with the cool attitude of plants
imprinted on the floor
truth is a pretty little varnish

Sleep is a small jar
filled with warm liquid, daytime
is a snail climbing up the tall pillar of
history
stretched out
climbing straight toward the wall-light of winter

Behind me, a heavy layer
of golden velvet
what is termed flora of the feminine
not a bronze revolving door to be had
here, nothing can be seen
nothing imagined

Locked outside, my little brother
on a flight of concrete steps

a staircase under a clear blue sky
cries
without a sound he cries
he's knocked over his bottle of orange soda

Crossing the Border

In the dust-covered street
it's God who lets you love
the bright and glistening sand
standing there, inspecting a handkerchief, it's
God who introduces you to the four of them
children, out of school, letting them
walk along beside you, giving you
clear directions, it's God
who lets you cherish the sand, pockets, and the children
holding tight to your hand to keep
the world from falling away

A wave, and another wave,
and the car
comes to a stop

Days Gone By

These days are not crying days
you live in a house of rain
but when you come out, you are dressed all in red
or we could say, red is everywhere

The suitcase remains behind when you move away
it lies in the field
shadowy field of wheat, where green birds rise and fall

from LIQUID MERCURY

5. THE FEEL OF THE WIND
The feel of the wind
reminds him of leaves
covering the lawns with biting lips
water-soaked lawns in
Shanghai
the hiss and slash of rain
covers the lawn
he keeps walking backward
listening to   the ringing, ringing
of little black beetles flipping over

     Morning   wedding
     biting each other's lips

Snow, snow white
blown backwards

Lifting oneself up
to see the new bride

6. WRITING BRUSH
Days in the wind
     all grow their hair long
     let it rain
     and push the front door open
     arranging the wedding
     changing dogs   pigs   and chickens

     Changing here, changing there

The eldest sister
is a whip
just now fallen in love
fifteen   twelve   fourteen seventeen

8. CORD
Backing away   bitten by a
wolf

Sent to a field hospital
eyes   alert
seen by a nurse
threaded by a needle
watching the glass melt

Stitched up so carefully
you put on an act of having stitches
exhausted
sometimes, with all the coming and going, they catch a glimpse of you

15. WILLOW JAR
With a small bumping sound
two people stand

              There is a city wall in the mountains
              there are trees near the wall
              there are women under those trees

Oh how their flowers   fade and fade some more
              eyebrows so delicate
              knives and clubs in hand

23. There're Not Many Birds in the Village Now

•

There're not many birds in the village now
not many at all
going outside to walk around

In the village there are some
and outside too

• •

Millet
falls to the ground
standing in the mud
cut down with a stroke
by the sickle in the wind

  •
• •

Pack full the rice basket for me

37. Aluminum Oxide
No one offered you a courtyard
where sometimes you'd see
pin-headed soldiers
standing beneath the trees

Apples fallen everywhere

A good many women
in seemingly good spirits
speak incomprehensibly
jabbering as they pass by
legs reflected in the water

Many flowers
two buds

39. Red Wheat
She sees her mouth hit the floor
she sees the bees rise and fall, up and down
there are many houses
hillside grasses from the hillside watch
she no longer has a mouth

She knows that smiles
are in the mind of the dead
sweet as examined throats
people who have died
seldom walk away alone

45. Solar Flare
Wheat grows from the earth
and so do poets
you watch the whole body revolve
birds flying off ahead
the heart of the precious stone
vague teeth marks in the ground

47. DEE DEE DA DEE DA

I.
Originally you could pass by
      clapping your hands
      walking across the lawn

Trees, bursting with leaves
you, bursting with words

Leaves

    Staying behind, you start the machine
bursts of bursts   bursting into smoke

II.
The overturned pail is seen from afar
      and dee da
    delicate fish
    dancing in the air

    Dee dee da dee da

Fish bring trees into the air
              dee da

Fish bring trees into the
         air
      rust-colored legs sticking up in the
                 air

III.
Dee dee da dee da

    Trees pump out smoke   start the machine

                                        trees
                                        overturn
                                        setting fish free

Dee dee da
            rapping, rapping on the pail, looking for some money there

You   rip slip by slip   slip by slip
         until the crystal snout is exposed

IV.
Dee dee da   dee dee da

            Turn the machine exposing the crystal snout
            a slip of a fish bursting into smoke

Five legs stuck out looking at me   at you
            we stare them down
            stare them down
            put them
                        down

V.
Dee da   dee da
         the overturned pail is seen from afar
         machine starting fish
         a slip of white fish
         placed in the fish dish
         slowly slowly   dancing
                                    into
                        the evening waves

      Stare them down

VI.

Rapping on the pail   looking for cash   and coins
                                          like evening fish

Water flows down clear and fast

Down below   a bus stop   moving house
ripping
        snouts

Afterward, taking care of things   climb to the sentry post high in the tree
                                                            dee da

VII.

        Legs stuck out   inside
                    watching
                    fish
                    in the wok
                    rain

The whole afternoon is the windy season

            The dish speaks   dishes
                                 dishes
                                 dishes

You're the only drop to leap from the pool
            the only one
            dee da

        The door is open, always swinging back and forth

48. A Minor God
On the business of moving mica
you say four   then you say forty

The Gaze

I.
They go upstairs
no one's there

When you open fire
don't forget the street of glittering flame

II.
Those on this side cannot go over to the other
and neither can those on the other side come here

None of the people crowded in the hallway can go to the other side

III.
This is true terror
burned-out houses
left standing like scraggly teeth

IV.
He stands up ahead
his collar red
you must salute
you must smile
you fret that you are too good-looking

V.
You are so frightening
smiling

Last time, it was not like this
LXXXIX
Year of the Snake

Oman

Under the windblown sea
there is a scuba-diving wife

Inside the uncrackable nut
there is the wind

Under the undamageable roof
there is a set of cards

Inside people who cannot love
there is the night

Under the staircase of soft fir that cannot be pushed
there are a foot   a clock   a stretch of waves
blown by the Second World War

Seven Days

I hope there will be someone
to see me off
    holding my hand

The crowds of people on the mountain slope
block the sun from view

Words

My dream won't last long
she has prepared fireflies

Anne Carson

THE TRUTH ABOUT GOD

My Religion
My religion makes no sense
and does not help me
therefore I pursue it.

When we see
how simple it would have been
we will thrash ourselves.

I had a vision
of all the people in the world
who are searching for God

massed in a room
on one side
of a partition

that looks
from the other side
(God's side)

transparent
but we are blind.
Our gestures are blind.

Our blind gestures continue
for some time until finally
from somewhere

on the other side of the partition there we are
looking back at them.
It is far too late.

We see how brokenly
how warily
how ill

our blind gestures
parodied
what God really wanted

(some simple thing).
The thought of it
(the simple thing)

is like a creature
let loose in a room
and battering

to get out.
It batters my soul
with its rifle butt.

The God Fit
Sometimes God will drop a fit on you.
Leave you on your bed howling.
Don't take it meanly.

Because the outer walls of God are glass.
I see a million souls clambering up the walls on the inside
to escape God who is burning,

untended.

The God Coup
God has a grand heart cut.
On the road where man surges along He may,
as the prophet says,
tarry.

By God
Sometimes by night I don't know why
I awake thinking of prepositions.
Perhaps they are clues.

"Since by Man came Death."
I am puzzled to hear that Man is the agent of Death.
Perhaps it means

Man was standing at the curb
and Death came by.
Once I had a dog

would go with anyone.
Perhaps listening for
little by little the first union.

Deflect
I have a friend who is red hot with pain.
He feels the lights like hard rain through his pores.
Together we went to ask Isaac.

Isaac said I will tell you the story told to me.
It was from Adam
issued the lights.

From the lights of his forehead were formed all the names of the
     world.
From the lights of his ears, nose and throat
came a function no one has ever defined.

From the lights of his eyes—but wait—
Isaac waits.
In theory

the lights of the eye should have issued from Adam's navel.
But within the lights themselves occurred
an intake of breath

and they changed their path.
And they were separated.
And they were caught in the head.

And from these separated lights came
that which pains you
on its errands (here my friend began to weep) through the world.

For be assured it is not only you who mourn.
Isaac lashed his tail.
Every rank of world

was caused to descend
(at least one rank)
by the terrible pressure of the light.

Nothing remained in place.
Nothing was not captured except
among the shards and roots and matter

some lights
from Adam's eyes

nourished there somehow.

Isaac stopped his roaring.
And my friend by now drowsy as a snake
subsided behind a heap of blueblack syllables.

GOD'S NAME
God had no name.
Isaac had two names.
Isaac was also called The Blind.

Inside the dark sky of his mind
Isaac could hear God
moving down a country road bordered by trees.

By the way the trees reflected off God
Isaac knew which ones were straight and tall
or when they carried their branches

as a body does its head
or why some crouched low to the ground in thickets.
To hear how God was moving through the universe

gave Isaac his question.
I could tell you his answer
but it wouldn't help.

The name is not a noun.
It is an adverb.
Like the little black notebooks that Beethoven carried

in his coatpocket
for the use of those who wished to converse with him,

the God adverb

is a one-way street that goes everywhere you are.
No use telling you what it is.
Just chew it and rub it on.

Teresa Of God

> "the aching has hold of me O grievous daimon"

Teresa lived in a personal black cube.
I saw her hit the wall each way she moved.
She cursed her heart

which was, she said, rent
and her nose
which had been broken again and again.

Some people have to fight every moment of their lives
which God has lined with a burning animal—
I think because

God wants that animal kept alive.
With her nose Teresa questioned
this project of God's.

To her heart God sent answer.
The autopsy after her death revealed
it was indeed rent.

Photographs of the event
had to be faked (with red thread and an old gold glove)
when the lens kept melting.

THE GRACE THAT COMES BY VIOLENCE
Yours is not (I regret to say) the story they tell
although you howl and gash yourself
scurrying out of the tombs

where you now live.
God forces some.
God's prophet came

to send your unclean spirit
into pigs, who ran amok.
I saw you

at the bottom of the cliff of pity
diving in pig blood—
"cleansed" now.

GOD'S WOMAN
Are you angry at nature? said God to His woman.
Yes I am angry at nature I do not want nature stuck
up between my legs on your pink baton

or ladled out like geography whenever
your buckle needs a lick.
What do you mean *Creation*?

God circled her.
Fire. Time. Fire.
Choose, said God.

GOD STIFF
God gave an onomatopoeic quality to women's language.
These eternally blundering sounds eternally
blundering down

into the real words of what they are
like feet dropped into bone shoes.
"Treachery" (she notices) sounds just like His zipper going down.

GOD'S BELOVEDS REMAIN TRUE
Chaos overshadows us.
Unsheltered sorrow shuts upon us.
We are strangled by bitter light.
Our bones shake like sticks.
We snap.
We grope.
We pant and go dry.
Our tongues are black.
All day is endless.
Nights endless.
Our skin crawls, it cracks.
Our room is a cat who plays with us.
Our hope is a noose.
We take our flesh in our teeth.
The autumn blows us as chaff across the fields.
We are sifted and fall.
We are hung in a void.
We are shattered on the ocean.
We are smeared on the darkness.
We are slit and drained out.
Little things drink us.
We lie unburied.
We are dust.
We know nothing.

We cannot answer.
We will speak no more.
BUT WE WILL NOT STOP.
For we are the beloveds.
We have been instructed to call this His love.

GOD'S BOUQUET OF UNDYING LOVE
April snow.
God is waiting in the garden.
Slow as a blush,

snow shifts and settles on God.
On God's bouquet.
The trees are white nerve nets.

GOD'S MOTHER
She doesn't get to say much in the official biography—
I believe they are out of wine, etc.,
practical things—

watching with one eye as he goes about the world
calling himself The Son of Man.
Naturalists tell us

that the hatching crow is fed by the male
but when it flies, by the mother.

Love	Fly	Man
Loves	Flies	Mans
Loved	Flew	Manned
Loving	Flying	Manning
Loved	Flown	Woman.

It is what grammarians call a difference of tense and aspect.

GOD'S JUSTICE
In the beginning there were days set aside for various tasks.
On the day He was to create justice
God got involved in making a dragonfly

and lost track of time.
It was about two inches long
with turquoise dots all down its back like Lauren Bacall.

God watched it bend its tiny wire elbows
as it set about cleaning the transparent case of its head.
The eye globes mounted on the case

rotated this way and that
as it polished every angle.
Inside the case

which was glassy black like the windows of a downtown bank
God could see the machinery humming
and He watched the hum

travel all the way down turquoise dots to the end of the tail
and breathe off as light.
Its black wings vibrated in and out.

THE WOLF GOD
Like a painting we will be erased, no one can remain.
I saw my life as a wolf loping along the road
and I questioned the women of that place.

Some regard the wolf as immortal, they said.
Now you know this only happened in one case and that
wolves die regularly of various causes—

bears kill them, tigers hunt them,
they get epilepsy,
they get a salmon bone crosswise in their throat,

they run themselves to death no one knows why—
but perhaps you never heard
of their ear trouble.

They have very good ears,
can hear a cloud pass overhead.
And sometimes it happens

that a windblown seed will bury itself in the aural canal
displacing equilibrium.
They go mad trying to stand upright,

nothing to link with.
Die of anger.
Only one we know learned to go along with it.

He took small steps at first.
Using the updrafts.
They called hi Huizkol,

that means
Looks Good In Spring.
Things are as hard as you make them.

GOD'S CHRIST THEORY
God had no emotions but wished temporarily
to move in man's mind
as if He did: Christ.

Not passion but compassion.
Com—means "with."
What kind of withness would that be?

Translate it.
I have a friend names Jesus
from Mexico.

His father and grandfather are called Jesus too.
They account me a fool with my questions about salvation.
They say they are saving to move to Los Angeles.

God's List Of Liquids
It was a November night of wind.
Leaves tore past the window.
God had the book of life open at PLEASURE

and was holding the pages down with one hand
because of the wind from the door.
For I made their flesh as a sieve

wrote God at the top of the page
and then listed in order:
Alcohol
Blood
Gratitude
Memory
Semen
Song
Tears
Time.

GOD'S WORK
Moonlight in the kitchen is a sign of God.
The kind of sadness that is a black suction pipe extracting you
from your own navel and which the Buddhists call

"no mindcover" is a sign of God.
The blind alleys that run alongside human conversation
like lashes are a sign of God.

God's own calmness is a sign of God.
The surprisingly cold smell of potatoes or money.
Solid pieces of silence.

From these diverse signs you can see
how much work remains to do.
Put away your sadness, it is a mantle of work.

Bei Dao

translated from the Chinese by Eliot Weinberger
& Iona Man-Cheong

June

Wind at the ear says *June*
June a blacklist I slipped
in time

note this way to say goodbye
the sighs within these words

note these annotations:
unending plastic flowers
on the dead left bank
the cement square extending
from writing to

now
I run from writing
as dawn is hammered out
a flag covers the sea

and loudspeakers loyal to the sea's
deep bass say *June*

Reading

Taste the unnecessary tears
your star stays
alit still for one charmed day

a hand is birth's
most expressive thing
a word changes
dancing
in search of its roots

read the text of summer
the moonlight from which
that person drinks tea
is the true golden age
for disciples of crows in the ruins

all the subservient meanings
broke fingernails
all the growing smoke
seeped into the promises

taste the unnecessary sea
the salt betrayed

Untitled

A trumpet like a sharp plow
tills the night: how long
till sunlight breaks the ground?

how long till those who listen respectfully
turn around and see us?
how long till we
through effort and exertion
turn into glory?

till the grain goes into the granary
this thought belongs to no one
a drop in the water-level between
this moment and the next life:
huge waves beat against the shore
next door to youth
we hear the wild palpitations

in a space even vaster
sleep stuffed with rice straw

Leaving Home

The compass jokingly
points toward a state of mind
you drink up the soup and leave
this scene of life

on the application form of
sky and electric wires, a tree
trembling to fly
so what can it write about?

no matter what happens, you'll
recognize the danger
a crowd of strangers sitting
at journey's end

at night the wind steals bells
the long-haired bride
quivers like a bowstring
over the body of the groom

Smells

Those smells making you remember again
like a horse-cart passing through the flea-market
curios, fakes, hawkers'
wisdom covered in dust

and there's always a gap between you and reality
arguing with the boss
you see the ad out the window
a bright tomorrow, Tomorrow brand toothpaste

you are facing five potatoes
the sixth is an onion
the outcome of this chess game is like sorrow
disappearing from the maritime chart

Postwar

Images distilled from the dream
abandon the flag at the horizon

the light cast by the pond
the laughter of those missing
makes it clear: pain
is the cry of the lotus

our silence
became straw pulp became
paper, that winter
healing the written wounds

Night Sky

Silent dinner
the dishes spin darkness
letting us share this
simmered anger
add a little salt

suppose there were an even greater
space—a stage
the starving spectators
looking up
at our acting

like raising a flag, rising into
the night sky: the square is shut down
a ray of light points out the changes
shifting planets
we begin to speak

Mission

The priest gets lost in prayer
an air shaft
leads to another era:
escapees climb over the wall

panting words evoke
the author's heart trouble
breathe deep, deeper
grab the locust tree roots
that debate the north wind

summer has arrived
the treetop is an informer
murmurs are a reddish sleep
stung by a swarm of bees
no, a storm

readers one by one clamber onto the shore

In Memory

Turning back from the end
when it was hard to breathe—
the angels of fallen leaves on the hill
the sea of heaving rooftops

on the way back to the story
the deep-sea diver in the dream
looks up at the ships passing by
blue sky in the whirlpools

the tale we are telling
exposes the weakness in our hearts
like the sons of the nation
laid out on the open ground

dialogue of wind and trees
a limp
we crowd around a pot of tea
old age

Moon Festival

Lovers holding pits in their mouths
make vows and delight in each other
till the underwater infant
periscopes his parents
and is born

an uninvited guest knocks at my
door, determined to go to deep
into the interior of things

the trees applaud

wait a minute, the full moon
and this plan are making me nervous
my hand fluttering
over the obscure implications of the letter
let me sit in the dark
a while longer, like
sitting on a friend's heart

the city a burning deck
on the frozen sea
can it be saved? it must be saved
the faucet drip-drop drip-drop
mourns the reservoir

Ramallah

in Ramallah
the ancients play chess in the starry sky
the endgame flickers
a bird locked in a clock
jumps out to tell the time

in Ramallah
the sun climbs over the wall like an old man
and goes through the market
throwing mirror light on
a rusted copper plate

in Ramallah
gods drink water from earthen jars
a bow asks a string for directions
a boy sets out to inherit the ocean
from the edge of the sky

in Ramallah
seeds sown along the high noon
death blossoms outside my window
resisting, the tree takes on a hurricane's
violent original shape

The Rose of Time

when the watchman falls asleep
you turn back with the storm
to grow old embracing is
the rose of time

when bird roads define the sky
you look behind at the sunset
to emerge in disappearance is
the rose of time

when the knife is bent in water
you cross the bridge stepping on flute-songs
to cry in the conspiracy is
the rose of time

when a pen draws the horizon
you're awakened by a gong from the East
to bloom in the echoes is
the rose of time

in the mirror there is always this moment
this moment leads to the door of rebirth
the door opens to the sea
the rose of time

NATHANIEL MACKEY

Song of the Andoumboulou: 46

Knowing of the world it
would remain without
   them, they lay entwined,
atavistic twins. Thick
                    weather
   crowded the room, thin
   limbs,   wood becoming
   watershed, stitchless,
                    warmed
each other's wintry
                    skin...
They lay entwined, asymmetric
   twins, each the other's
long lost remnant,   each
   in what seemed like speaking
   mounted skyward, each
                    the
   other's complement, coughed
   up a feather, watched it
                    float...
They lay entwined, atavistic
twins, empty streets ran thru
   their heads, they lay on their
                    backs.
   Dark what once had been lit,
   deserted city,   arrived but
   without what advantage might
                    accrue,
came to where they'd been before,
   what there'd been before now

no longer there…They lay
  entwined, asymmetric twins,
                              swung
tangent to one another's turning,
    whatsaid its indiscreet regress…
  Unarrested regret roaming the
    warmth and the smell of their
                              skin,
    residue of heaven, his her
  insurmountable ridge too high to
  be reckoned, Anuncia's wrecked
arcade unveiling joint flesh bunched
  under cloth…   Not not having
                              gone
    not having gone far enough, not
                              not having
    known how far enough went, west of New
Not Yet,   night was a mountain
    looming high, too tall to envisage,
  Anuncia's wrecked arcade reconnoitered,
                              reeled,
      whatsaided
      back

                    •

A river they thought they saw winding
snakelike. Looked at from an airplane
    window, sun bounced up from under,
                              blinding
      white… Taken aside, I sat beside
        them, an aisle seat, same row,
      snakelike what up close would've only
        been water…   So now no longer
                              was her

name Anuncia. Nunca was the new one she
      took. Never to be seen again, twinless,
unentwined, turned away, went, her

                              straught
         body wound wavelike, never to be
         lain with again… Wound wavelike,

                                   snakelike,
         looked at from ersatz heaven, having so
         lain recollected, began again to say

                              goodbye…

Said wait but to what avail might've said
      nothing, Nunca's raw kiss gone away
      as though winged… As we as well were,
         however many we were, so many dead

                                   borne
      about, not yet without soul albeit

                              all
   but so

                     •

   They lay on their backs looking
up at the sky treading light, lies
      put away they thought. Moist eyes
      he'd have drowned in, likewise
         the wet of her mouth.
                              Took
         between her legs his want of
respite unannounced… A nonsonantet
      it was he dreamt he'd someday play

                              in,
an unstrung lute he'd someday pluck…

I pulled him aside to say braids
unravel, a meddler to my chagrin.
                              "'So
        Night sits me down before...,'" he
                              began
        but broke off, knew I knew what came
next. "I sistren," I said, not yet knowing
        what I said, myself no more the he than
                                        the

                she of it regardless... Regardless,
                I pulled him
                aside

                ——————————————

        Prodigal rift an aroused we tossed
        off, I was what was left. Talk made
        my lips move,   fishlike...   I was
the remnant I fought the feeling I
                              was...
        So it was that countlessness turned
        my head, made it spin. Two meant
                more than I could say.   I sat to one
side, beside myself,   mounting light
                                        folded
        in at more removes than I could count,
        counting farther off to the side than
        even I was, number now beside the
                                        point...

        The Abdominal Two I was tempted to call
        them, off to my left looking out at
                                        the

world, belly's rub wrangled and again

                                         begun

to flare

––––––––––––––––––

(brayed)

Something we saw we only said we
saw we thought at first, not saw
  but made believe we saw we somehow
      thought,   Nunca sat on a see-thru
  throne. Inside the room
                which
was all window our legs gave out…
    An altar the floor seemed,
                  receding,
  fell away, fell from the knees
    dropped down on to meet it,
    chivalric, no longer there.
                  To
    want was to risk it, not no
  guarantee, see no more than say
                 made

so

––––––––––––––––––

It was a tale told many times over,
muttered under one's breath unintended.
All the songs had long been sung.

Might've been bass, might've been
  guitar, strung so tight we tore

wood from its neck... So that
                    what I
wanted was what there was, Earth a
                         ball of
    dust and water... All the songs
        had long been sung,   numb choir,
                              sandpaper

    coating our
    throats

Song of the Andoumboulou: 56

    At long last we came to the
    Dread Lakes region, graduating
    body and bone. It wasn't we
so much as web we were, buh,
                    the
        implied increment, zuhless,
                         web,
        no zuh, no buzz... Got there
    at long last thru a maze of
    cities, quaint faces arrayed
    on balconies along the way.
                         Matted
    hair dotted the ground as we
strode in, the earth itself quick
        with feeling, sentient,
                         felt
        it rub the soles of our feet...
        It was a march we were on, a
        campaign, carnival trek
    translated of late and of late
        what before had been ruse
                         become

real. It was a float we were
    on it appeared, a layer of light
  between the ground and the soles
    of our feet... It wasn't we were
                            prey,
  buzzing fly, flying fish,   wasn't we
    were inside Ananse's web, Anuncia's
net. Web it was we were, it wasn't
      we were caught. It wasn't we
      were web's, we were web...

                        Invisible
  lips blew ripples on the water, vatic
    breath blown wordless, the exegete's
bequest, endlessly expended wind. The
                          lakes'
      faces fraught with import, splay
  auspice's day begun. Day wet with
    allegorical water, rebegun,
                          endlessly
  repeated, dreamt amendment's end, lakes
      looking back at us it seemed. Faces
  we'd seen in cities we saw again,
                          watery,
all but undone... It wasn't Babylon where
      this was nor its outskirts, dread
  faces captive kin,   furrowed lakes
    where before they'd been featureless,
                          blank
but for the exegete's bequest. Fraught or
      without furrows, Fret Lakes either
  way, Dread Lakes all the same... Dread
  Lakes lay southeast of everywhere,
endlessly down and to the right. The
                          farther

they receded the deeper we were there,
apart from where we otherwise were…
Got there in trucks or simply walked,
it wasn't clear. Dread Lakes had it that
                                        way…

   Dread Lakes lakes in name only rife with
names, names' unthinkable dearth. Fret
Lakes, Dearth Lakes, Dare Lakes like
bone, Bone Lakes' alibis… Lakes rubbed
raw by strung voices, parched earth what
                                        before
   had been mud. Mud what before had
      been water, Dread Lakes fiery dry…
   It was a furnace we were in, dotted
      bodies eventually blent, Dread
   Lakes' evaporative largesse. Blent
                                        we
   partly were. Web it was we were. Blent
                                        was
   web's distant
kin

                •

   The waterless lakes they turned out to
be turned us back. Turned away, we
   turned inward, buoyed against our
   will, better to've sunk we thought…
Thought we thought, we admitted,
                                        abstract
      baptists, glad to be dry, undunked…
   An adamant canvas it turned out
      we were on, polychromatic

powders, dust. Dotted bodies
                         begun
    to be other than bodies, half-again
     themselves not themselves…
                           Kissed,
   otherwise moistureless, caressed,
    hands and fingers finding their
way. It wasn't grope what we did,
                        we
decrypted,   bulge and declivity were
                          code…

   Desert love, bedouin strand at lake's
edge, into it before we knew where. Signs
all around, how to read them none of us
    knew. It wasn't we were lost, we lost
    track absorbed as we were,   recondite
                          recess,
   crevice, fold… Immersed in what wasn't
there, desiccant slough what was, toward
and away were now one. Code even
   so, siphoning substance… Dread
                     Lakes
   alias, cavewall inside out,   dotted
    bodies bespoke "immanent elsewhere,"
half-again "all but already gone." Why
                     we
   became web was no conundrum, why
buh wasn't buzz no zuh… Pelvic Hollow
    it was we now called it, come upon as
                        drift,

  dry
  run

Dried up if so much as looked at, dreamtime
equation of body and lake, down under
    lay intangibly above… We stood
    on the lake's bed, what was left
                    of it,
  wished-for new beginnings no beginning,
    the new world we expected up in
smoke. Again gave thought to the
    he and she we saw embrace, etched
    andoumboulouous forms we saw
                    in the
    dirt, thought we saw Rorschachwise…
                      Moved
  among landmarks whose names were
    legion, Rock-the-Spotted-Lizard-Passed-
      Wind-On, Fallen-Tree-Where-the-
      President-Spat… Ledge-Where-
      the-Bramble-Tore-Pant-Legs come
                  to last,
    color clung to our feet. Drift,
    aboriginal forage… Abject
    endlessness, abstract arrest… Color
claimed our feet, drawn-out exit,
                  dreamt
  amenity, endlessly
 cathectic
trek

●

What would accrue to color kept us
afoot. Paints and pastels lay in our
    way… We the painted ones ran, feet
        wet, canvas rent. Blue rabbits
        we might've been… Namesake
                                    hair
    was what shrubs and brush were,
                            the lakes'
        eponymous locks. Dread Lakes was
    the name it all went by, lake floor baked
    by unremitting sun, low scrub and brush
were brown. Scrub was what covered the
                                    ground
        and what we did, endlessly abraded earth
    rayed out around us, endlessly scratched-at
sky… Hedge-the-Judge's-Pay-Lay-Hid-Behind
    lay to our left. Withered-Creek-the-Wounded-
        Bird-Left-a-Feather-In loomed up
                            ahead…

    A sonorous canvas it became as we
advanced. Blown reeds accosted us
    with wind raising dust. Grit got into
        our nostrils, eyes and throats… An ill
        wind in the dead of August, blown
                            reeds
    laid us out on a cooling board… It wasn't
we were dead or that the world was, wasn't
        we bid anything goodbye. It was the
        all-in-all otherwise known as web and it
                            relaxed
    us. Grit was web's alias, web in scrub disguise,
scrub's atomistic reach… We made up ground

in a
made-up landscape, no less real for that...
Wind on us hard as it was we ran even faster.
                                        Stride

was our true country, native
                    ground

————————————

Abstract canvas, earth tones notwithstanding.
Color clung to our feet. Caved alias, pelvic
    alcove, under intangibly above...
  Knotted highness lay on the ground
                                in

clumps we tripped over, lakes and
    canals come to in dreamtime,
    intricate fingers braiding love's
                            true
locks. Dread Lakes it was nonetheless,
                        Dredge
  Lakes were it under lay visibly above,
Dram, Drawn Lakes it was, Dread Lakes
    all the more even so. Dread Lakes was
  where we were, where we'd been, where we'd
    be. Dread was the color claimed our feet...
                            Might've
    been saffron or something like henna, red-
  brown, yellow-brown, spiked earth at the
                            soles
    of our feet, heels and the
    balls of our feet
    pestling
light

A worked awkwardness ran us over. "We
don't care" popped out of our mouths. Stomp
  got our feet, ran up our legs, trunks, necks,

                              put a

    big Foot up the sides of our skulls…
    Anticlimactic we called it, disconsolate,
  paint put on us by the way we came
    thru, scrub's perimetric net. A step
short of web's edge, nothingness. More

                          than

    could be come to, caught. It wasn't
  as we'd said, wasn't we were free, wasn't
    as we'd said about buzzing fly, flying fish,

                          wasn't

  we were wingless, web's it
  was we
were

82

MICHAEL PALMER

The Words

The birds with bones of glass:
perhaps the terror will end

in a flowering tree in July.
The book lying open in the light,

the book with mottled spine,
all possible information inside:

Riemann hypothesis resolved,
the zeta and zeros, entry 425;

The Paradox of the Archer
on the succeeding page;

the lost language of moths
a little further along.

Slow wing beats of owls
down the book's corridors.

Sky a cadmium yellow
from the fires to the north.

They seem to follow us, the fires,
as page follows page.

The bones, the birds, the glass, the light, the primes;
book, words, zeros, fires, spine.

Construction of the Museum

In the hole we found beside the road
something would eventually go

Names we saw spelled backward there

In the sand we found a tablet

In the hole caused by bombs
which are smart we might find a hand

It is the writing hand
hand which dreams a hole

to the left and the right of each hand

The hand is called day-inside-night
because of the colored fragments which it holds

We never say the word desert
nor does the sand pass through the fingers

of this hand we forget
is ours

We might say, Memory has made its selection,
and think of the body now as an altered body

framed by flaming wells or walls

What a noise the words make
writing themselves

for E. H.
11 apr 91

"or anything resembling it"

The hills like burnt pages
Where does this door lead

Like burnt pages
Then we fall into something still called the sea

A mirrored door
And the hills covered with burnt pages

With words burned into the pages
The trees like musical instruments attempt to read

Here between idea and object
Otherwise a clear even completely clear winter day

Sometimes the least memorable lines will ring in your ears
The disappearing pages

Our bodies twisted into unnatural shapes
To exact maximum pleasure

From the view of what is in any case long gone and never was
A war might be playing itself out beyond the horizon

An argument over the future-past enacted in the present
Which is an invisible present

Neva streaming by outside the casement
Piazza resculpted with bricolage

Which way will the tanks turn their guns
You ask a woman with whom you hope to make love

In this very apartment
Should time allow

What I would describe as a dark blue dress with silver threads
And an overturned lamp in the form of a swan

A cluster of birches represents negativity
Flakes of ash continue to descend

We offer a city with its name crossed out
To those who say we are burning the pages

Autobiography 2 (hellogoodby)

The Book of Company which
I put down and can't pick up

The Trans-Siberian disappearing,
the Blue Train and the Shadow Train

Her body with ridges like my skull
Two children are running through the Lion Cemetery

Five travelers are crossing the Lion Bridge
A philosopher in a doorway insists

that there are no images
He whispers instead: Possible Worlds

The Mind-Body Problem
The Tale of the Color Harpsichord

Skeleton of the World's Oldest Horse
The ring of O dwindles

sizzling around the hole until gone
False spring is laughing at the snow

and just beyond each window
immense pines weighted with snow

A philosopher spreadeagled in the snow
holds out his Third Meditation

like a necrotic star. He whispers:
archery is everywhere in decline,

photography the first perversion of our time
Reach to the milky bottom of this pond

to know the feel of bone,
a knuckle from your grandfather's thumb,

the maternal clavicle, the familiar
arch of a brother's brow

He was your twin, no doubt,
forger of the unicursal maze

My dearest Tania, When I get a good position in the courtyard
I study their faces through the haze

Dear Tania, Don't be annoyed,
please, at these digressions

They are soldering the generals
back onto their pedestals

for A. C.

Una Noche

Then El Presidente,
uncoiling his tongue,

"You cannot stop time
but you can smash all the clocks."

And so, seeking Paradise,
we have burned the bright house

to the ground.
A necessary act.

We have invented glass
and ground a dark lens

and in the perilous night
we continue to dance.

The tarantella, the tango,
the passadoble and the jig,

the bunnyhop, the Cadillac,
the Madison and sarabande,

mazurka and the jerk,
the twist on tabletops.

Rolling our eyes,
flailing our limbs.

It's how we keep time,
our feet never stop.

I Do Not

Je ne sais pas l'anglais.
Georges Hugnet

I do not know English.

I do not know English, and therefore I can have nothing to
    say about this latest war, flowering through a night-
    scope in the evening sky.

I do not know English and therefore, when hungry, can do no
    more than point repeatedly to my mouth.

Yet such a gesture might be taken to mean any number of
    things.

I do not know English and therefore cannot seek the requisite
    permissions, as outlined in the recent protocol.

Such as: May I utter a term of endearment; may I now proceed
    to put my arm or arms around you and apply gentle
    pressure; may I now kiss you directly on the lips; now
    on the left tendon of the neck; now on the nipple of
    each breast? And so on.

Would not in any case be able to decipher her response.

I do not know English. Therefore I have no way of
    communicating that I prefer this painting of nothing to
    that one of something.

No way to speak of my past or hopes for the future, of my
    glasses mysteriously shattered in Rotterdam, the statue
    of Eros and Psyche in the Summer Garden, the sudden,
    shrill cries in the streets of São Paulo, a watch
    abruptly stopping in Paris.

No way to tell the joke about the rabbi and the parrot, the
    bartender and the duck, the Pope and the porte-cochère.

You will understand why you have received no letters from me
    and why yours have gone unread.

Those, that is, where you write so precisely of the
    confluence of the visible universe with the invisible,
    and of the lens of dark matter.

No way to differentiate the hall of mirrors from the meadow
    of mullein, the beetlebung from the pinkletink, the
    kettlehole from the ventifact.

Nor can I utter the words science, seance, silence, language
    and languish.

Nor can I tell of the arboreal shadows elongated and shifting
    along the wall as the sun's angle approaches maximum
    hibernal declination.

Cannot tell of the almond-eyed face that peered from the
    well, the ship of stone whose sail was a tongue.

And I cannot report that this rose has twenty-four petals,
    one slightly cankered.

Cannot tell how I dismantled it myself at this desk.

Cannot ask the name of this rose.

I cannot repeat the words of the Recording Angel or those of
the Angel of Erasure.

Can speak neither of things abounding nor of things
disappearing.

Still the games continue. A muscular man waves a stick at a
ball. A woman in white, arms outstretched, carves a true
circle in space. A village turns to dust in the chalk
hills.

Because I do no know English I have been variously called
Mr. Twisted, The One Undone, The Nonrespondent, The
Truly Lost Boy, and Laughed-At-By-Horses.

The war is declared ended, almost before it has begun.

They have named it The Ultimate Combat between Nearness and
Distance.

I do not know English.

Dream of a Language that Speaks

Hello Gozo, here we are,
  the spinning world, has

it come this far?
  Hammering things, speeching them,

nailing the anthrax
  to its copper plate,

matching the object to its name,
  the star to its chart.

(The sirens, the howling machines,
  are part of the music it seems

just now, and helices of smoke
  engulf the astonished eye;

and then our keening selves, Gozo,
  whirled between voice and echo.)

So few and so many,
  have we come this far?

Sluicing ink onto snow?
  I'm tired, Gozo,

tired of the us/not us,
  of the factories of blood,

tired of the multiplying suns
  and tired of colliding with

the words as they appear
    without so much as a "by your leave,"

without so much as a greeting.
    The more suns the more dark—

is it not always so—
    and in the gathering dark

Ghostly Tall and Ghostly Small
    making their small talk

as they pause and they walk
    on a path of stones,

as they walk and walk,
    skeining their tales,

testing the dust,
    higher up they walk—

there's a city below,
    pinpoints of light—

high up they walk,
    flicking dianthus, mountain berries,

turk's-caps with their sticks.
    Can you hear me? asks Tall.

Do you hear me? asks Small.
    Question pursuing question.

And they set out their lamp
    amid the stones.

                for Yoshimasu Gozo

The Thought

We breathe in, we do not think
of it. We walk and we speak

beneath the blue-flowering trees
and do not think. We breathe.

We cross the stone bridge
above a fisherman in a skiff.

We pass the blind man, the legless man
and the woman who sings of a coming storm.

We sit by the river in the rising wind,
we raise the crazed cup to our lips

and do not think,
here where the light does not differ from dark,

here where pages tumble to the floor,
here in the lake of ink, the stain of ink

where we fashion a calendar from a wall.
Invisible lake, unreachable shore.

Exhale and do not think.
Close their eyes a final time close our eyes.

to Faraj Bayrakdar

Homero Aridjis

translated from the Spanish by George McWhirter

Self-Portrait at Six Years of Age

A pane of glass separated Altamirano hill
from my hands.

Beyond, the classroom door shut out
a stair that plunged into the town.

Everything wanted into Spanish class:
the ash tree, the stones, the sparrow, the blue of the sky.

Frayed dress and tongueless shoes,
my pencil drew the country schoolmarm.

I learned to read like we learn how to be:
you, me, father, brother, the shadow on the wall.

A Wounded Self-Portrait

I
Birds just passed over
the white sky of the house.
I stare up into the striae
of a cancelled noon.

2
The silence has split lips
and a red geranium has come in through the window.
I grab the shotgun, as one grabs death by the torso.
My face, a fugitive in the mirror.

3
The birds have flown across the sky in the mirror.
My eyes won't let them go
off, into the forgotten. They want to
do yesterday over in the void.

4
I climb up a pile of bricks.
My eyes tangle in the bougainvillea.
I hoist the shotgun at the bodies flying.
Aim the shot away into another blue.

5
Like an azure shadow,
the smallest bird goes at the fore.
All gone are the calls
and I didn't kill one.

6
I point the shotgun
at myself. Noon
has me dazed. I slam
the butt on the ground.

7
I feel the hot blood
and the air explodes.
My body's a bursting
powder cap in space.

8
To catch hold of me, a servant girl
opens her arms. As if leaping
into the bosom of death I leap
toward her.

9

I don't fall. Hugging me she carries
me to my room and puts me on the bed.
In come my parents, frightened.
Noon smells of gunpowder.

10

Out of the foul mouth of a bar
comes a pop song:
'Soon as she saw me sad, she was for staying,
but already the news was written, her love that night I'd lose.'

11

I can't really say. I have lost
the love of no one. I have
found it. A cat chases
skinny shadows over the roof.

12

From this moment on I will be someone
else. Another me.
Poetry has me won over.
I am flying, stretched out on the bed.

13

With words I will buy time
With words I will buy death
With words I will buy words
With words I will paint the day white.

Self-Portrait at Age Ten

In the schoolyard,
girls with fat legs
are playing house.

With wooden swords
the boys play at slaying each other,
slicing their short little shadows.

Standing, wan
and unsociable, atop a stone,
I follow my eyes down into the town.

There is my house. There
I am, pointing a shotgun
at the birds I love so much.

Suddenly, my belly is riddled.
I am the centre of all the beauty.
I've written my first poem.

Self-Portrait at Eleven on a Train

Glued to the window,
my face reflected the sad glass.
The train of life was leaving behind
passes, precipices and dust.

Even though his being sat elsewhere,
my father was there, eating an apple in front of me.
The few passengers appeared lost,
as if they already belonged to the forgotten.

On walls, the light pasted up distances
as if the sun were shunting by in memory.
Aboard the train, your life swept into an abyss,
face glued to the sad glass.

Self-Portrait at Thirteen Years of Age

Of myself, a survivor
I sit on the barber's chair.

On a stand is the mirror,
beyond that, the hillside.

I stare at the tongues of my old shoes
on the footrest.

The chair springs nip at my back.
Chon parts my hair with the comb,

crosses my head with snips of the scissors,
pitching off clumps onto the cobblestones.

Vanityless, flies sunbathe on the cobbles
or stick to Chon's brow.

He puts them to flight with a twitch of his ears.
The village smells of manure and roses.

The barber shows me his masterpiece:
a perfect bowl-cut.

In the hand mirror
I see the sun setting on the hill.

'I will sing the light,' I say to myself,
feeling I am a poet already.

Self-Portrait at Age Sixteen

He smokes his first Tiger
between the pines on Altamirano;
the town lies at his feet, a sleeping
body of adobe and tile.
Lank, longhaired,
beardless, he makes love
to everything: lark, oak,
the butterfly and the distance.
The days skip by without name or date,
ignoring the cage of hours,
the same as a desire
that could take shape anywhere.
There below, the streets
are an open hand
between whose fingers
the sun plays at
throwing its knives.
On the ridge the yap
of a fox is heard, a hind's bleat;
drunk on green rain
his eyes enter the underbrush.
The sun yellows his face,
paints his hands with its setting.
He leaves his shadow between the pines,
his Tiger, crushed out on the ground.

Self-Portrait at Fifty-Four Years Old

I am Homero Aridjis,
I was born in Contepec, Michoacán,
I am fifty-four,
with a wife and two daughters.

In the dining room of my house
I had my first loves:
Dickens, Cervantes, Shakespeare
and the other Homer.

One Sunday afternoon
Frankenstein came out of the town movie
house and on a stream's bank
held out his hand to a boy, who was me.

The Prometheus pieced out of human remnants
went on his way, but since then,
out of that encounter with the monster,
the verb and the horror are mine.

Self-Portrait in the Doorway

You go into your parents' house
to visit your childhood
and the handle of the door
comes loose in your hand.

You go down the hall
that took you to your room
and find shadows
seated on the benches.

There's an indoor garden
in the room where you slept
but how skinny the bed is
and chilly, the walls.

Street cries
no one sees or hears
come in through the broken window
with the air, the night.

Your mother is dead now.
Your father is dead now.
In the pear tree no one picks the pears,
no one reads the paper in the doorway.

Your childhood home
is a paradise in ruins.

Aharon Shabtai

translated from the Hebrew by Peter Cole

Nostalgia

> *Shall I weep if ... an infant civilization*
> *be ruled with rod or with knout?*
> —Tennyson, *Maud: A Monodrama*

The dumpy little man
with the scourge in his hand,
in his free time
runs his fingers
over the keys of a baby grand—
but we've seen it all before.
And so, from the primitive East
we return to the West.
He'll help solve the economy's problems:
the unemployed will man the tanks,
or dig graves,
and, come evening,
we'll listen to Schubert and Mozart.
O my country, my country,
with each sandal,
with each thread
of my khaki pants,
I've loved you—
I could compose
psalms to a salad
of white cheese and scallions.
But now, who will I meet
when I go out for dinner?
Gramsci's jailers?
What clamor will rise
up through the window facing the street?

And when it's all over,
my dear, dear reader,
on which benches will we have to sit,
those of us who shouted "Death to the Arabs!"
and those who claimed they "didn't know"?

Rosh HaShanah

Even after the murder
of the child Muhammad on Rosh HaShanah,
the paper didn't go black.
In the same water in which the snipers
wash their uniforms,
I prepare my pasta,
and over it pour
olive oil in which I've browned
pine nuts,
which I cooked for two minutes with dried tomatoes,
crushed garlic, and a tablespoon of basil.
As I eat, the learned minister of foreign affairs
and public security
appears on the screen,
and when he's done
I write this poem.
For that's how it's always been—
the murderers murder,
the intellectuals make it palatable,
and the poet sings.

Our Land

I remember how,
in 1946, hand in hand
we went out into the field
at the edge of Frishman Street
to learn about Autumn.
Under the rays of the sun
slanting through the October clouds
a *fallah* was cutting a furrow
with a wooden plough.
His friend wore a *jallabiya*
rolled up to his knees
as he crouched on a knoll.
Soon we will all
meet in the Tel Aviv below—
Weinstein the milkman,
and Haim the iceman,
Solganik
and the staff at the dry-goods co-op:
Hannah and Frieda and Tzitron;
and the one-armed man
from the clothing store
at the corner
near Café Ditza;
Dr. Levova
and Nurse Krasnova;
the gentle
Dr. Gottlieb.
And we'll meet Stoller
the butcher,
and his son Baruch;
and Muzikant the barber,
and Lauterbach, the librarian;
and the pretty dark-skinned lady

from the Hahn Restaurant.
And we'll meet the street-sweeper
Mr. Yaretzky,
whose widow had hanging
in her hallway
the parable-painting
showing the stages of life.
For these *fallahin* as well,
and also for the children of the village of Sumel,
who herded goats
on Frug Street,
the heart will make room
like a table
opening its wings.
For we belong
to a single body—
Arabs and Jews.
Tel Aviv and Tulkarem,
Haifa and Ramallah—
what *are* they
if not a single pair of shoulders,
twin breasts?
We quarreled
like the body parts of the man
who brought the milk of the lioness
down from the mountains
in the legend told by Bialik.
Through the cracks in the earth,
we'll look up at you then;
under your feet
our land is being harrowed
with chains of steel,
and above your heads there is no sky
like a light-blue shirt—
but only the broad buttocks of the murderer.

Basel Square

After months abroad,
I strolled down to Basel Square
and the store run
by the grocer from Wadi Ara.
That same smile
on a devastated face
flickered at the edge
of a shopkeeper's mouth,
or a barber's,
along Alexanderplatz
during the thirties.
With a feeble grip like this
they shook the hands
of clients,
members of the master race,
who deigned to drop in.
And this is what drives
the sleep from my eyes
and forces me
to rise and go back to the table
in this dim hour
when the thud of the paper
hitting the doorstep is heard.

Hebrew Culture

Hebrew culture resembles
two sisters,
both good girls,
who married soldiers,
career officers—
one called Pinkie,
and the other Bougie.
Early each morning,
Pinkie and Bougie rise.
One runs around
with platoons of artillery,
sowing death
among the poor,
destroying homes
over old and young;
and the other gazes
out through a pair of binoculars,
gradually cutting
a village in half
where groves had flourished,
and turning entire cities
into concentration camps.
From a distance of ten kilometers,
nothing is heard but the sound of sprinklers.
Books are put back on the shelf
within their handsome jackets,
and the two sisters
turn to their respective recipes
and start to cook:
one makes goulash for Bougie,
and the other—pasta for Pinkie.

Hope

It's hopeless, you told me,
waking in the middle of the night—
the moonlight drifting
in through the curtain—
and you looked at your wife,
at her thin, whitening shoulders
and dark hair
as she was slowly breathing,
thinking again and again
of all this evil,
the loss amassed in the soured heart
day after day, for two years and more.
It was in Karmei Avdat.
I rose, you said,
and without my glasses
went out barefoot onto the gravel
to a bench we'd moved
against the shed
and sat there in my underwear,
staring out toward the side of the hill.
Along that slope, I told you,
five million stones have been cast:
the stones will always be stones,
no good will ever come
of them or to them—
not in another two years,
and not in a hundred.
But if you shift your eyes
even a meter to the side,
you'll see a plant
with five tomatoes.
That's where you should look.
These vile people

will acquire
plane after plane
and bomb after bomb,
and more will be wounded and killed,
more be ruined and uprooted;
for this is all they're capable of,
and not tomorrow, and not forever,
will any good come
of them or to them,
for evil holds no promise
and possesses neither the life nor yield
contained in a single tomato.
When I think of this land,
love flows through my heart.
When I think of Amira and Neta,
and Rachel in her orange parka—
and not of the pus of the cruel
or their barking,
and their *boom boom boom*—
but this substance,
this certain serum
that's secreted in me
and throughout the world gives rise
to building, repair, and enlightenment,
counsel and cooperation,
this is the hope
that lends me a place and ground
in which to send out a bold root
there, beyond that heap of stones
at the Mas'ha checkpoint,
at the store run by the old grocer
with the white crocheted-cap
who stands by the door
with plates of *labneh*
which he takes out of the rickety fridge;

and this is the longing and yearning
to go down into the village groves
and through the breach in the barbed-wire fence,
to cross the ditch—
turning my back
to the land-grabbers' contractor
who, with his guards,
peers out from the jeep
at the burrowing bulldozer—
and like someone in Florence
climbing to the top
of Brunelleschi's Dome,
to mount that hill
and under the tree beside the tent,
to sit with Riziq and Nazeeh,
to look into Nazeeh's face
at his toenails and black sandal,
to see Riziq's cigarette—
this is hope—
and with Nazeeh and Riziq
to look out far beyond the fence,
beyond the barbarity,
toward the border of humanity.

Sharon Resembles a Person

Sharon resembles a person,
and the imminent peace resembles peace,
and the paper reporting with fanfare
resembles a paper,
and teachers resemble teachers,
and education—education.
From the window of bus #5
I look out at people along the sidewalk,
accompanying them in my mind,
and all of it only confirms
that they resemble people—
the shoes, the falafel, the mouthful,
et cetera.
At the grocer,
with trembling fingers
I check the potatoes,
and they too, they too,
resemble potatoes.

As We Were Marching

Two days ago in Rafi'ah,
nine Arabs were killed,
yesterday six
were killed in Hebron,
and today—just two.
Last year
as we were marching
from Shenkin Street,
a man on a motorcycle
shouted toward us:
"Death to the Arabs!"
At the corner of Labor,
opposite the Bezalel Market,
next to Braun's
butcher shop,
and at the corner of Bograshov:
"Death to the Arabs!"
For a full year
this poem was lying
on the sidewalk
along King George Street,
and today
I lift it up and compose
its final line:
"*Life* to the Arabs!"

SUSAN HOWE

Silence Wager Stories

When I come to view
about steadfastness
Espousal is as ever
Evil never unravels
Memory was and will be
yet mercy flows
Mercies to me and mine
Night rainy my family
in private and family

I know I know short conviction
have losses then let me see why

To what distance and by what path
I thought you would come away

———————

1
Battered out of Isaiah
Prophets stand gazing
Formed from earth
In sure and certain
What can be thought
Who go down to hell alive
is the theme of this work
I walk its broad shield
Every sign by itself
havoc brood from afar
Letting the slip out
Glorious in faithfulness
Reason never thought saw

2
You already have brine
Reason swept all away
Disciples are fishermen
Go to them for direction

Gospel of law Gospel of shadow
in the vale of behavior
who is the transgressor
Far thought for thought
nearer one to the other
I know and do not know
Non attachment dwell on nothing
Peace be in this house
Only his name and truth

3
Having a great way to go
it struck at my life
how you conformed to dust
I have taken the library
Volumes might be written
ambiguous signs by name
Near nightfall it touches it
Nothing can forbear it
So fierce and so flaring
Sometimes by the seaside
all echoes link as air
Not I cannot tell what
so wanton and so all about

4

Fields have vanished
The Mower his hopes
Bow broke time loose
none but my shadow
she to have lived on
with the wood-siege
nesting in this poem
Departed from the body
at home of the story
I'm free and I'm famished
And so to the Irish
Patrol sentinel ensign
Please feel my arms open

5

The issue of legitimation
Identity of the subject
Circumcision of a heart
driven outside its secret
Elysian solitary imagination
by doubt but not by sight
Fear that forever forever
perfect Charity casts out
The Canticle is an allegory
unchangeable but changeable
Fluttering robes of Covetous

He is incomprehensible he
makes darkness his covert

6
Ages pre-supposed ages
the darkness of life
out of necessity night
being a defense by day
the cause and way to it
From same to the same
These joining together
and having allegiance
Words are an illusion
are vibrations of air
Fabricating senselessness
He has shattered gates
thrown open to himself

7
Though lost I love
Love unburied lies
No echo newlyfledge
Thought but thought
the moving cause
the execution of it
Only for theft's sake
even though even

perturb the peace
But for the hate of it
questionless limit
unassuaged newlyfledge
A counter-Covenant

8
Mysterious as night itself
All negligently scenery
if Nothing could be seen
Sacraments are mysterious
Ambiguous in literal meaning
the Pentateuch the Angels John
all men form a silent man
who wrote the author down
Sackcloth itself is humility
a word prerogatives array
Language a wood for thought
over the pantomime of thought
Words words night unto night

9
Drift of human mortality
what is the drift of words
Pure thoughts are coupled
Turn your face to what told me
love grazed here at least

mutinous predominant unapparent
What is unseen is eternal
Judgments are a great deep
Confession comes to nought
half to be taken half left
From communion of wrongdoing
doubleness among the nouns
I feed and feed upon names

10

Claim foreign order
dismantling mortal
Begotten possibility
plummet fetter seem
So coldly systems break
Fraught atvantaging
Two tell againstself
Theme theme heart fury
all in mutiny
Troubleless or sadder
Estranged of all strange
Let my soul quell
Give my soul ease

11

Antic prelate treason
I put on haircloth

Clear unutterable
Secret but tell
What diadem bright
Theme theme heart fury
Winged knowledge hush
Billeted near presage
such themes do quell
Claim foreign order
Plummet fetter seem
wild as loveDeath
Two tell against self

12

Strange fear of sleep
am bafflement gone
Bat winged dim dawn
herthe midmost wide
I did this and I
But forever you say
Bafflement nether elegy
herthe otherwise I
Irreconcilable theme
keep silent then
Strange always strange
Estrange that I desire
Keep cover come cover

13

Lies are stirring storms
I listen spheres from far
Whereunder shoreward away
you walked here Protector
unassuaged asunder thought
you walked here Overshadow
I listen spheres of stars
I draw you close ever so
Communion come down and down
Quiet place to stop here
Who knows ever no one knows
to know unlove no forgive

——————————

Half thought thought otherwise
loveless and sleepless the sea
Where you are where I would be
half thought thought otherwise
Loveless and sleepless the sea

INGER CHRISTENSEN

translated from the Danish by SUSANNA NIED

from ALPHABET

1
apricot trees exist, apricot trees exist

2
bracken exists; and blackberries, blackberries;
bromine exists; and hydrogen, hydrogen

3
cicadas exist; chicory, chromium,
citrus trees; cicadas exist;
cicadas, cedars, cypresses, the cerebellum

4
doves exist, dreamers, and dolls;
killers exist, and doves, and doves;
haze, dioxin, and days; days
exist, days and death; and poems
exist; poems, days, death

5

early fall exists; aftertaste, afterthought;
seclusion and angels exist;
widows and elk exist; every
detail exists; memory, memory's light;
afterglow exists; oaks, elms,
junipers, sameness, loneliness exist;
eider ducks, spiders, and vinegar
exist, and the future, the future

6

fisherbird herons exist, with their grey-blue arching
backs, with their black-feathered crests and their
bright-feathered tails they exist; in colonies
they exist, in the so-called Old World;
fish, too, exist, and ospreys, ptarmigans,
falcons, sweetgrass, and the fleeces of sheep;
fig trees and the products of fission exist;
errors exist, instrumental, systemic,
random; remote control exists, and birds;
and fruit trees exist, fruit there in the orchard where
apricot trees exist, apricot trees exist
in countries whose warmth will call forth the exact
color of apricots in the flesh

7

given limits exist, streets, oblivion

and grass and gourds and goats and gorse,
eagerness exists, given limits

branches exist, wind lifting them exists,
and the lone drawing made by the branches

of the tree called an oak tree exists,
of the tree called an ash tree, a birch tree,
a cedar tree, the drawing repeated

in the gravel garden path; weeping
exists as well, fireweed and mugwort,
hostages, greylag geese, greylags and their young;

and guns exist, an enigmatic back yard;
overgrown, sere, gemmed just with red currants,
guns exist; in the midst of the lit-up
chemical ghetto guns exist
with their old-fashioned, peaceable precision

guns and wailing women, full as
greedy owls exist; the scene of the crime exists;
the scene of the crime, drowsy, normal, abstract,
bathed in a whitewashed, godforsaken light,
this poisonous, white, crumbling poem

8
whisperings exist, whisperings exist
harvest, history, and Halley's

comet exist; hosts exist, hordes
high commanders, hollows, and within the hollows
half-shadows, within the half-shadows occasional

hares, occasional hanging leaves shading the hollow where
bracken exists, and blackberries, blackberries
occasional hares hidden under the leaves

and gardens exist, horticulture, the elder tree's
pale flowers, still as a seething hymn;

the half-moon exists, half-silk, and the whole
heliocentric haze that has dreamed
these devoted brains, their luck, and human skin

human skin and houses exist, with Hades
rehousing the horse and the dog and the shadows
of glory, hope; and the river of vengeance;
hail under stoneskies exists, the hydrangeas'
white, bright-shining, blue or greenish

fogs of sleep, occasionally pink, a few
sterile patches exist, and beneath
the angled Armageddon of the arching heavens, poison,
the poison helicopter's humming harps above the henbane,
shepherd's purse, and flax, henbane, shepherd's purse
and flax; this last, hermetic writing,
written otherwise only by children; and wheat,
wheat in wheatfields exists, the head-spinning
horizontal knowledge of wheatfields, half-lives,
famine, and honey; and deepest in the heart,
otherwise as ever only deepest in the heart,
the roots of the hazel, the hazel that stands
on the hillslope of the heart, tough and hardy,
an accumulated weekday of Angelic orders;
high-speed, hyacinthic in its decay, life,
on earth as it is in heaven

9
ice ages exist, ice ages exist,
ice of polar seas, kingfishers' ice;
cicadas exist, chicory, chromium

and chrome yellow irises, or blue; oxygen
especially; ice floes of polar seas also exist,

and polar bears, stamped like furs with their
identification numbers, condemned to their lives;
the kingfisher's miniplunge into blue-frozen

March streams exists, if streams exist;
if oxygen in streams exists, especially
oxygen, especially where cicadas'
i-sounds exist, especially where
the chicory sky, like bluing dissolving in

water, exists, the chrome yellow sun, especially
oxygen, indeed it will exist, indeed
we will exist, the oxygen we inhale will exist,
lacewings, lantanas will exist, the lake's
innermost depths like a sky; a cove ringed
with rushes, an ibis will exist,
the motions of mind blown into the clouds
like eddies of oxygen deep in the Styx

and deep in the landscapes of wisdom, ice-light,
ice and identical light, and deep
in the ice-light nothing, lifelike, intense
as your gaze in the rain; this incessant,
life-stylizing drizzle, in which like a gesture
fourteen crystal forms exist, seven
systems of crystals, your gaze as in mine,
and Icarus, Icarus helpless;

Icarus wrapped in the melting wax
wings exists, Icarus pale as a corpse
in street clothes, Icarus deepest down where
doves exist, dreamers, and dolls;
the dreamers, their hair with detached
tufts of cancer, the skin of the dolls tacked together

with pins, the dryrot of riddles; and smiles,
Icarus-children white as lambs
in greylight, indeed they will exist, in-
deed we will exist, with oxygen on its crucifix,
as rime we will exist, as wind,
as the iris of the rainbow in the iceplant's gleaming
growths, the dry tundra grasses, as small beings

we will exist, small as pollen bits in peat,
as virus bits in bones, as water-thyme perhaps,
perhaps as white clover, as vetch, wild chamomile,
banished to a re-lost paradise; but the darkness
is white, say the children, the paradise-darkness is white,
but not white the same way that coffins
are white, if coffins exist, and not white
the same way that milk is white, if milk exists;
white, it is white, say the children,
the darkness is white, but not
white like the white that existed
when fruit trees existed, their blossoms so white,
this darkness is whiter; eyes melt

10
June nights exist, June nights exist,
the sky at long last as if lifted to heavenly
heights, simultaneously sinking, as tenderly as
when dreams can be seen before they are dreamed; a space
as if dizzied, as if filled with whiteness, an hourless

chiming of insects and dew, and no one in
this gossamer summer, no one comprehends that
early fall exists, aftertaste, afterthought;
just these reeling sets of restless ultrasounds
exist, the bat's ears of jade

turned toward the ticking haze;
never has the tilting of the planet been so pleasant,
never the zinc-white nights so white,

so defenselessly dissolved, gently ionized and
white, never the limit of invisibility so nearly
touched; June, June, your Jacob's ladders,
your sleeping creatures and their dreams exist,
a drift of galactic seed between
earth so earthly and sky so heavenly,
the vale of tears so still, so still, and tears
sinking, sinking like groundwater back

into earth; Earth; Earth in its trajectory
around the sun exists, Earth on its journey
along the Milky Way, Earth on its course with
its cargo of jasmine, jasper, iron,
iron curtains, omens, jubilation, Judas's kiss
kissed right and left, and virgin anger in
the streets, Jesus of salt; with the shadow of the
jacaranda over the river, with gyrfalcons, jet planes,
and January in the heart, with Jacopo della Quercia's
well Fonte Gaia in Siena and with July
heavy as a bomb, with domestic brains
heart defects, quaking grass and strawberries
the ironwood's roots in the earthworn earth

Earth sung by Jayadeva in his mystical
poem from the 12th century, Earth with
the coastline of consciousness blue, with nests where
fisherbird herons exist, with their grey-blue arching
backs, or where bitterns exist, cryptic
and shy, or night herons, egrets,
with the wingbeat variations of hedge sparrows, cranes

and doves; Earth exists with Jullundur, Jabalpur and
the Jungfrau, with Jotunheim, the Jura,
with Jabrun, Jambo, Jogjakarta,
with duststorms, Dutchman's breeches
with water and land masses jolted by tremors
with Judenburg, Johannesburg, Jerusalem's Jerusalem

atom bombs exist

Hiroshima, Nagasaki

Hiroshima, August
6th, 1945

Nagasaki, August
9th, 1945

140,000 dead and
wounded in Hiroshima

some 60,000 dead and
wounded in Nagasaki

numbers standing still
somewhere in a distant
ordinary summer

since then the wounded
have died, first many,
most, then fewer, but

all; finally
the children of the wounded
stillborn, dying

many, forever a
few, at last the
last; I stand in

my kitchen peeling
potatoes; the tap
runs, almost
drowning out the
children in the yard;

the children shout,
almost drowning out
the birds in the
trees; the birds
sing, almost

drowning out the whisper
of leaves in the wind;
the leaves whisper,
almost drowning
the sky with silence,

the sky with its light
and the light that almost
since then has recalled
atomic fire
a bit

11
love exists, love exists
your hand a baby bird so obliviously tucked
into mine, and death impossible to remember,
impossible to remember how inalienable

life, as easily as chemicals drifting
over the knotgrass and rock doves, all of it
is lost, vanishing, impossible to remember that
there and there flocks of rootless

people, livestock, dogs exist, are vanishing;
tomatoes, olives vanishing, the brownish
women who harvest them, withering, vanishing,
while the ground is dusty with sickness, a powder
of berries and leaves, and the buds of the caper
are never gathered, pickled with salt
and eaten; but before they vanish, before we
vanish, one evening we sit at the table with
a little bread, a few fish without cankers, and water
cleverly turned into water, one of
history's thousands of war paths suddenly
crosses the living room, you get up, limits,
given limits exist, streets, oblivion

everywhere, but your hideout comes no nearer
see the moon is too brightly lit and Charles's Wain
is going back empty as it came; the dead want
to be carried, the sick want to be carried, the broken
pale soldiers looking like Narcissus want to
be carried; you wander around in such a strangely
endless way; only when they die do you stop
in a kale patch no one has tended for several
centuries, follow the sound of a dried-up
spring, somewhere in Karelia maybe, and as
you think of words like chromosomes and chimeras
and the aborted growth of lychees, fruits of love,
you peel off some tree bark and eat it

somewhere I am suddenly born
in an expressionless house; when you
cry out the walls give way and

the garden, in which you vanish, is
worn smooth by slugs; you bathe
jerking like a bird, and when the earth

is eaten and the rhubarb first
dries up, summer gives way and
the town, in which you vanish, is

slow and black; you walk in
the streets, do as others do,
wordlessly in passing nudge

bits of brick into place; when the route
is tenacious, ingrained enough, the houses
give way, and the high plain spreads,

sullen, almighty, and almost
invisible; somewhere a wild
apricot tree stands still for a moment

and blooms, but just with a very
thin veil on the outspread branches
before going on regardless

fragment of a springtime, the kind
of evening when the roads lead almost
off into the blue, but no one
moves; the dust of the roads recalls
the dust of the roads where most
are shot and the silence
tugs at stones, but nothing happens

somewhere something no one has
touched tumbles from a shelf,
perhaps as my grandmother stands
as she always has stood in her
kitchen and cooks up dried apricots;
I know she is dead, but their scent
is so strong that the body sensing it

it becomes fruit itself; and as
the fruit is hung up in the nearest
tree, which may be a birch that
bears catkins, never apricots,
the shot sounds beforehand, ahead
of just after, its sound like a
door with no house standing wide open still

hydrogen bombs exist
a plea to die

as people used to die
one day in ordinary

weather, whether you
know you are dying
or know nothing, maybe

a day when as usual you have
forgotten you must die,
a breezy day in

November maybe, as
you walk into the kitchen
and barely manage to

notice how good
and earthy the potatoes
smell, and barely

manage to put the lid on,
wondering whether you
salted them before you
put the lid on,
and in a flash,

while puffs of steam
leak past the lid, barely
manage to remember your life
as it was and still
is, while the potatoes

boil and life, which you
always have said must go
on, really does go
on, a plea, an
ordinary plea, an

ordinary day, that
life can continue
completely ordinarily
without it ever happening
that any of all

the cruel experiments
that the Teller group
performed on
Eniwetok where
the waves of the
Pacific raged in fury,
or any of all
the experiments that

the Sakharov group
performed on
Novaya Zemlya where
the waves of the Arctic
Ocean raged in fury
without these
experiments or those
of the British French

Chinese ever reaching
real real-
ization here where we
still live in a
real real
world as opposed to
the unreality of
Novaya Zemlya

and Eniwetok; here I
walk down to the still
blue of the Sound shining
with evening, toss
a stone into the water,
see how the circles
widen, reaching
even the farthest shores

Gustaf Sobin

Fourteen Irises for J.L.

there, blossoming once again, like blown
goblets, the irises in their annual
    ovulations.   yes, emptiness, at
last, enveloped, inscribed.   is there anything, indeed, but
        emptiness?   but emptiness, at last, en-
               veloped? inscribed?

—————————————

. . . one color
follows upon another like
    polyphonic voices: last week, violet, and
this, a rubbed mahogany, freckled rose, recalling
        worlds —voices— you've never known.

—————————————

. . . like so
many stubby paintbrushes, they
    burst —turbaned— into splashed
panels, running murals (a breath as
        if perishing in the
          very exercise of its scales).

—————————————

no, it's not the irises that
return, each spring, but
    ourselves.   ourselves —cyclical— who've entered the

sign, and stoop, now, before
                them: tenuous altars to our own
                                tenuous passage.

---

                        all irises, finally,
                        kaleido-
                        scopic; with each
                        in-
                        finitesimal turn, a
                        fresh

                        conceit.   god-
                        blossom, lightning-

                        root, verb on which,
                        germinal, the
                        air it-

                        self's as if
                        ir-
                        idized.

---

    like those glazed, in-
voluted tissues on their tall, un-
        wavering stems, we, too, as if
    perch, alighting —as we have— amongst phonemes,
                polyphones: what tell us, each
                                instant, to our fingertips.

---

came late.   even later, now, *la*
langue d'oc having all
    but vanished, remained the irises, the troubadours'
lightning roses, blue
        as thunder in the dark thunder's
            dissoulucioun.

---

      where dew slips,
      icy
      pearl, from its

      petal, the
      tall stalk

      scarce-
      ly trembles. . . .

---

irises, really, are nothing more
than the frozen frames of an otherwise
    invisible drift, our relentless
elision past.   what they —heraldic,
        voluptuous— would arrest.

---

how each of these blossoms —these
volutes— lapping ogival, in-
    scribe a void.   oh ours, that hollow, that
      heart, that inherent omission: doom blooming
        from the rhizomes up.

---

drafted, the petals get blown, now,
across paper.   their deep
     scrolls, rolled tabernacles, little more
               than scribbled deposits.   chimeric hoards.

(gothic)

death, and these,
our ever

more
ephemeral re-

sponses, their
fluttering
chalices (faience
the

skull dreamt . . .).

. . . way that the irises drift, now, be-
neath yours.   current in which —wind-
     barges— they'd enter, perhaps, your
very dreams.   there, before dissolving (so much
     grammatical particle) might billow.   writhe vibrant.

----

a white chair, its legs caught
in tall stalks
    of white iris, was what, finally,
  remained.   monologue in which, abandoned
                      to those immensities, each
                         of us murmur.

Anguish & Metaphor

only in air
  do the knots dissolve, only
without, with-
in, in the echoing

organs, dis-
perse.   earth in-

verted, a life as if passed
a-
mongst its
attributes, you'd rise,
rise as

I'd plummet, your hair —in-
voluted— harden, just
there, where

I'd
vanish.

On the Nature of the Iconic

what bursts in the very moment of bursting is image.

its bunched chimera.

even though, immediately after, she'd as if begun gather-
ing together her every gesture; as if collecting —once
again— the scattered, grey blades of her gaze.

accumulating —as you'd put it— diaphanous.

just there, where the curtains ripple, each time, through
the draft of their own deafness.

neither this side, nor that.

(of what, indeed, knew no end, no depth, no dimensions
whatsoever, but —being verbless— existed in an under-
world entirely its own).

a well of shadows —you might have written— surrounded
by a garland of splashing leaves.

by the gloss of so much apparent matter.

while she —steadily— as if thinned into focus.

(fixed rays of her earrings; what she'd just fastened, sap-
phire).

muscled, luminous.

as if such signs (in an uninterrupted emission of signs)
might only have erupted out of the disarticulated.   its
depths.

cast in so much counterpart.

she, as if reconstituting that white memory to which you'd
otherwise have had no access.

miming its exact outlines, its deepest cleavages.

toying, thus, with those immemorial losses, thoroughly un-
aware, in so doing, of the magnitude of such provocation.

the tips of her fingers, that very instant, running nimble
over her glowing cheeks; adjusting here, there, the slight-
est wires of that all-too-perfect dissemblance.

like notes, struck vibrant, off some dismantled instrument.

yes, just then, as her each feature converged.   grew limpid.

the circumstantial, absolute.

oh, all the meanings, values, irrefutable definitions we'd
given ourselves.

the alphabets.   the blown letters of how many driven al-
phabets.

(within which, notwithstanding, had adored).

as she stood there, now, her name changing with the light,
the shadows, the time of day: pure replica of the otherwise
obliterated.

as if the door alone might be altar.   our very last.

and the moment itself, sacrificial.

Sixth Ode: The Grottoes

is always towards the furthest, and,
   finally, towards the
lost themselves that the senses transit, slip
furtive.   that bunched in
muscle, we'd

lusted, it seems, after so
very

little.   channels, conduits, the
   secret history —perhaps— of history it-
self, written
in

dark drafts, elusive
scribbles.   as if, inadmissible, mass in its
very
densities, were
riddled.   and you, nothing more

than this breath
that edged.   tongue that
in-

sinuated.

             ~

                    oh eyes so pale, you'd
written, they'd
promised grottoes.   oh holy, the

grottoes, the hollows, the weird birds of
our own,
dis-

articulated heart.   (what, in
de-

fault, had
been plundered,
re-
lentless).

~

'an earth, but else-
where,' isn't this
what you meant?   what you'd say?   what the
eyes rising —yes, so pale,
    so
impervious— already divulged?   for *here*'s
only here in the vocable's
forced

re-
tention.   past, past
ourselves, in our own, sonorous dis-

persions, resonates the
gloriole, the
ring

of things released.   the rocks, just
now, as if a-
float

in the puddle of their own shadows, and the
papery, pink blossoms of the
cistus, rife

with light, with the very
light, it would

seem, of some ultimate
ac-
quittance.

                         ~

massed, now,
a-
long the edges, awaited —you'd written— no,
not the barge, the puffed
barge, but the

particle.   but the
predicate, be-

fitting.

                         yes, holy the grottoes, the
hollows, those extricated worlds which
lie, luminous with
sound, there —just
there— past the inviolable lines of

our own
fore-

closures.

ROSMARIE WALDROP

from HÖLDERLIN HYBRIDS

IV. UNACCOUNTABLE LAPSES

I

What is memory? A palace? The belly of the mind? Of absence a dream? The baby in the picture I don't remember, but I remember my doll.

▲

Knowledge with a flavor of thin air. The more invisible the fabric befits neighboring particles. But the sun's eaten in the sky and still. Its own body keeps. And where it is we pursue. So more like a piece of property to which I lay claim. Than a state of mind. Or androgyny. Or love of black pepper.

▲

In dark ivy I sat. In the shade of an oak. Just as noon poured down and lost wax. In my ears loitered. According to tradition. A shadow fell across clear-cut narration as I followed Wittgenstein to places. Where nothing happens.

▲

Even as I let wander my thoughts. The way blood cells circulate to any part of the body. Or birds keep hopping. From branch to branch. Which makes them hard to keep track of. Unless I have words that don't fall. Between the tracks.

▲

How many times can one single heart beat? So many breaths deep and shallow. While the years pass without hard edges. So I could put them end to end.

2

Animals do not hunt for a story. But blind am I in my soul. A fault is embedded. And were it not for the doll I would not. Know who I am. A pocket in space expanding less rapidly.

▲

A riddle is anything pure. In pure memory (what is pure memory? and where?) I might know my image. But not find a caption. Though a name of my own I have no matter what time of year.

▲

So should I inward turn? Breath held long enough to show. The rim of vertical time. Molecules into slower vibrations betrayed. A flake of death off the skin.

▲

Do we remain as we begin? Not to words then would thinking turn but to our first soaking sunlight. To rage raw and desperate cleaving the body. Like lightning the earth.

▲

So where must I search for my childhood? Among folds of the brain at the risk of falling between? Or in my throat an acid reflux? In order to repeat? What to complete I have failed? Until there's a hole in the window where I meant to toss the stone?

3

Maybe the past is enough for the past and all its inhabitants. They need not be drawn out of retirement. But if I repeat without knowing I repeat? Am I in my own body?

▲

Or is the past, like the Gods, without emotion? and gropes for our feelings lest it transparent turn? Like a woman not looked at? Fading between the pages of Grimms' Kinder- und Haus-Märchen?

▲

Meanwhile breath by breath down burns the house and under its rubble buries us. And great bodies of thought melt away. And no form identical to them ever again on the face of the earth appears.

▲

Though of love and sweet of summer traces float through arteries like great ships. Carrying kits for survival since the body is practical. And only when the brain's defenses are down, as in dreams, do we drown in the pure stream.

▲

The way Madame Blavatsky dipped her body in the Ganges and, says Yoel Hoffmann, said a prayer for plants. And did not consider the history of the earth and its reigns of silence and long sleep.

4

Not every fish has a jaw and many are the soft-bodied beasts our ancestors. And many forgotten beyond the shale of recall. Though their history can be read, some claim, in the cells of our body. The way language contains the layers of its development.

▲

And Dante said angels have no need of memory for they have continuous understanding. But we. To enter into thought. Need a bridge.

▲

But a mind obsessively drawn toward memory. Its own obstacle becomes. Like magnets pushed apart by the field they create. Or I enter the picture as a shadow because dumbly I get in the way of the light. And because I am shadow I cannot see.

▲

Or the way we cut open. Heads and x-ray our chests. In the effort to find love.

▲

Clustered on the tip of my tongue. Are names of species. Intermediate links that heard with their skin. Now missing for lack of. Or other reasons. While we improbable and fragile too. Head toward extinction.

▲

Not hard-shell certain the outcome in the match. Of recaller and recalled. And may alter both beyond recognition. Property is not passive.

5

Sudden the song of the blackbird and touches buried desire. You are there in the sound. What goes on in the soul that we must understand and can't?

▲

If the eye were a living creature, says Aristotle, its soul would be its ability to see.

▲

Skin stretches below the subconscious. The song gathers. In their straying flight. Lines that carry the weight of absence.

▲

This is a thirst that resembles me.

.

V. AT THE SEA

I

Down to the shore. And smell of brine. Away from moss, fern, mortar, brick. Form is fatal, some say. Whereas an endless unborn surface. Without point. Of reference. Containment. Or even vanishing.

▲

Here where the light is. Less hidden? Less dispersed into less things? Rolls in. White-crested. Splendor after splendor. Wall piled on wall. High as a house. And down comes crashing. Rocks. Severed heads. Centuries. And from the sand a thin veil of white recedes. And ripples and shadows and a ledge of clouds lined orange.

▲

Seeing is believing. But unthreatened by the dark are words. And there take refuge. Unshadowed. And thinking too takes refuge and then its own seed of light tries to sow.

▲

Pounding pounding the waves. Breath skyward drawn. Out of observable space, of muscular intuition. And the light goes on pretending that seeing is simple. That with mine own eyes have I touched. The shell in the sand. The fin of the minnow.

▲

I know the creed of light. We see. On condition of not seeing. The light. Transparent we dream the immediate.

2

With such amazing speed the eye. Of Ted Williams, say. Makes contact with the ball. It does not seem tied to its body. Does this reveal the nature of vision?

▲

Out at the sea I stare. As if it were the universe. Could pull the infinite into my eye. Without the rational lines of perspective. With absent wavelengths represented as imagination. Slow the eye I brought with me from Germany. And does not leave its body. Nor change the stance of distance.

▲

Blue. Two kinds of. Gray. Immersion. Open. Foam. Hallucination?

▲

Not toward. Not where I came from. No home beyond hard the sky limit. Away then? Seeing is leaving? The Western profile? The country whose mechanisms I understand no better than the light? And which. Like the light. Pretend they're not there.

▲

We come to a limit and stop. If there is no limit we cannot distinguish. Lost and no longer. I and everything else.

▲

Eyes breathe. Like open wounds.

3

Monet writes a friend he's painting "the instant." Succession stopped at success. A light his palette gives off. And color subdivided into into. On the retinal surface. Ground so fine. In each ray of light. Move motes of dust.

▲

Vibrations. Speed. Weather. Whatever blue.

▲

The killifish slip out of sight. Out of my mind: Sunrise. Tequila. "Ännchen von Tarau." Nails growing. Axons and dendrites. The dentist. My mother's maiden name. The ordinary physical scale.

▲

And how to talk to. I don't know. The dead. We've drained the symbols so our stories be cool. But it would take. The depth of years we stand on. The sea. Frequencies out of range. And air. Insurmountable its lack of resistance.

▲

Which I breathe in and breathe out. And commit my tongue to mate with the nick of time. And like a dream bone worry it. And the sound of the words has no measurable size.

▲

Eyes wide open. Retinal warp. Into the distance where it stops. Being distance. The brain turns pale and like to freezing. The body takes a long time to reassemble itself.

4

Out of the word came the light. On the first day of creation. Introduced separation. From the dark. And time. In alternation.

▲

The light took time. In its headlong flight. And knotted it into space. Where we pursue happiness, always belated. But the light did not remain. Unknotting the dimensions back it went. Into the word. And time's left with nothing.

▲

Or the light neither returned nor issued. And needs no justification. But in the swells there's memory. Between crest and trough. Of great upheavals.

▲

Refracts words. The light. Into runaway decay, instant loss. We make do with coins. And wish for slower language. Of darkness an eyeful. More local colors.

▲

Eyes cross the frontiers of glass. Penetrating. Penetrated. Like lovers. And like lovers rocked loose from the ground. By the grammar of convergence or some other force. Bloodstream pulled out to sea.

▲

Before slowed circulation and red sleep.

5

High tide. High above my head the water level. Rising. And thoughts float on it. Out of my depth. Their number displacing their weight. Movement in all directions, not going anywhere. A desk on the Atlantic.

▲

Eye without lid. Absorptive like a sponge of undecided sex. But I'm not made for all worlds.

▲

The light falls. On. Like the eye. And lingers. While its unseen colors try to penetrate under. The skin, for instance. And are blocked by the opaqueness of the body.

▲

Inward the nails grow later and the mind turns on itself. Myopic poison. And great ships sail over dry land.

▲

There is no clemency in the light. Or in the dark.

Gennady Aygi

translated from the Russian by Peter France

Again: Air in the Tops — Of Birches

lighter:

:

freedom:

:

(of old)

House—In the Grove of the World

house – or world
where I went down to the cellar
a white day it was – and I
was going to get milk – a long time it lasted
going down with me: it was
day – like a river: of brimming
expansion of light
leaping into the world: I
was the creator of an event
in the age
of firstcreations –

to the cellar – long ago – it was simple longlasting –

the grove white in the mist
and this
child with a pitcher – eyes a universe – and heaven
sang in all its breadth – like a special song
spread over the world
by women – simply shining in the movement
of its whiteness – into the expansion of the field
where in voice I was beginning –

to be – a universe-child:
I was – for it sang and it was

Supper: House Outside Town

1

even the sugar is murmuring: "and do you remember how they came for you – how they came at dawn" – although now the disaster is another – and the thought now is not of that

2

someone was saying "I" someone whispered "bread": "this is sleep-and-family" – clashed fleetingly in far-off singing: I leant-and-stiffened – as if rising somewhere like a burning pillar amid others in an ancient festive-field: to cast myself out from the chorus of those who move . . . –

— and later a line was traced – in blood! –

and then I saw – from another hidden chorus: of people-suffering – from forgotten depths flaring up in the brain – and perhaps in the memory of body-as-soil: to forget in secret – I saw children (and with dawn was mingled "I-am-sleep-and-family": like singing – with light! – with a wound in the temples – like a mouth)

3

"how then you walked" – this quiet thing keeps on murmuring – "how then you walked through the grove"

House in the Field

all very simple: a mouse – rubbish quivering
and wind round the corner
and there – a road in the rain at night
and just here – in the garden – a table
abandoned: and the talk – all sidelong and aslant
clinging and rustling
of familiar (like an old jersey) leaves
and homeland-mist – ever more ever nearer
with the soul-glance – of long gone long gone
(how can I speak it) mother . . . –

– here the bell of the Tyrol sings out
itself alone: riv-ver: all wide open
like purest blood. . . . . –

swallow in hiding and mouse
call out to the heart: you shut the door
and with twilight of soul in the house
feeling your way . . . – so the world is ended:

closed up – with a long forgotten whisper

Two Epilogues

I
cleanness of the path
simplicity of water —

and such a sky — as if a dream
of this height — unknown to all
very — oh yes very — different
bright poverty of Earth —

speaking a little to us

"while we are in the world
smoke — in cottage chimneys — plays"

2
something hospital-dimly-white
in the field slid and shifted
— God grant us this quietness cure us —
and the road out of the window as if beyond gates
was fading ever damper more sadly
"there" as if whispered "is all our earthly road"

Fields of this Summer

and even here
time seems to tremble – again renewing
these farewell-fields –

(like peoplefarewells) –

now they stretch out like tremulous darkness
(in something ever more
earlier – than childhood) –

now – stumbling in soul's unevenness
you awaken in the grass – as in memory
someone's departedness –

(and the grasses spill out
the last speaking) –

and the rustle – the scraping (somewhere a digging
of someone underground . . . no: it is nearer:
"it is
the heart growing old") –

and then – as if they had just
opened a window
on the path –

and clouds over grasses
make a universe . . . –

they seem
to move – to rise up!

as if all this
Builds-and-Chants – the inviting Harmonious
somewhere
Breathing –

and concluding – so we too must fall silent:
"far off" – it is only a quiet sound
of a distant homeland . . . (oh yes: like a hymn. . .)
and this
is straightway
long ago

This August's Phloxes

now – I cannot get warm: slowing
with their calmness – my steps! . . . –

– and the wor-rk of mo-ur-ning went on
(long ago – in their featherlight world. . .) –

and what – more detailed – can I tell you? –

but that – you yourself – invaded – with a distant cry:

. . . with that storm unseen I shall stay . . . –

until when? – . . . you run stretching out hands:

oh whiteness! . . . oh dissolve – into yourself! –

(separate the tears on the face)

From Lines in a Dream

and with the left side of the face
looking aslant
honestly directly
the pallor – in a dream – of Shostakovich
sacrificially – crying
as through fractured mud –

as if – to a friend

Quietness with a Happening

1
her islands

2
and again – it grows dark:
this is human-quietness
(how strange) without danger

3
and – (with nobody) – light

4
again – the movement
of her islands

During a Friend's Illness

it seemed a dream of God – and now a memory
folding into a Vision forgotten (now falling apart now
    beginning again)
of snow on faraway hills and roads
of children's speech-clothing
of animals' faces of smile-and-weeping – close by – on the
    threshold of friends:
of you – my dears: oh, painting, life,
Recent-Inexpressible
(beautiful like a poor man's meal)

Day – Towards Evening

And they float out and are fixed
and settled – these Stacks
of the end – of the coming
Millennium (. . . convention of a moment . . .) – and the Setting Sun's
magnificence
steadfastly – meanwhile – abides – and soon the immortal
Seal of the Road
openly settles itself – visibly-slowly:
on the edge of the forest – for ever – to Shine

Beginning from the Field

all day — the wind's repetition
of itself
from the edge — of the nearby field:

visibly — lightly — widely! —

but here — among peasant
buildings
its stumbling steps
ever deeper — like a meeting
with "Someone" — of the soul! —

no clarity — no distinction

The People Are a Temple

And souls are candles, each lighting the other.

HANS FAVEREY
translated from the Dutch by FRANCIS R. JONES

EIGHTEEN POEMS

*

The vase
I am holding in my hands
and carrying to the kitchen
to fill with water

lacks neither the vase
it is and will be, nor

the vase which a moment ago
bursts into flames once again,
and only then dashes itself
to pieces on the ground.

*

The muffled thud with which the strange cat
lands in the room, and wakes me.
While she carries on sleeping

I look at the cat. This cat knows
I'm seeing it. The same moonless
night that on Hadrian's Wall

a snowy owl is sitting, motionless:
until the cat suddenly begins
to lick itself all over and I must have
shifted position. Are you awake?
(Shssst.) Go away cat.

Extremely slowly the snail
crosses the path, and before
she knows it she is saved.

But in the undergrowth,

where the leaves are,
where it is cool,
the consummation awaits her:
to be absorbed into a greater
whole, a drier, swifter creature.

*

What it is all about,
I repeat, is
next to nothing.

A tiny dun spider,
with a tinge of rust,
which I cautiously approach
with my forefinger, suddenly
jumps almost a meter
away from me.

If the opening were forever
pierced by the opened,
nothing would remain in the end
but the same, fanning out
till night strikes, declares that

enough is enough. If someone
should choose his death: whose
chosen one is he, through
whom does he shudder thither?

Love dons her black cap
and kills. Even an onion surrenders
all in the end. Just as a chair, in spite
of everything, everywhere and nowhere,
wishes only to sit in for itself.

*

More fleeting than my shadow is,
the myrtle has no scent. No man
can manage to be more fragile
than the mortal inside me.

As soon as I am summoned, I come
into being in order to disappear.
Love serves the forgetting; the shirt
the wind has left behind will not

fit me. I usually have to
do what I want so that I
may die as befits me.

*

Although is is forever
itself, it constantly has to
be summoned. To this end
I summon and I am summoned.

The work whose end I serve
must make headway;

if not—the grasses will wither,

the mountain collapse, the tent
it lives in blow away, water
begin to burn as far as the horizon,
till in the end reigns only absolute
memory of hissing perfection,
forever self-voiding oblivion.

*

As a woman might
give or not give herself,

in calculation, in love;
a maple leaf have long begun
its fall, or have not quite
let go its branch;

the drops of water on my lips
how mindful of their river still,
its flow—but no longer of
the sea of clouds, so self-enlacing
in their billows, so self-effacing.

*

Why did she not stay where she is,
if she is not here and would rather
have gone there than be as one
with what remains when all

is destroyed: letting herself

slip onewards just as she is:
an almost beautiful beautiful woman
balancing on the edge of herself,
trying to convince me she exists

just because I'm lying in her arms

in which I've never been lying,
nor ever will, anyway.

*

The train scarcely slackens speed
and he is there: much the same man.

Now he is standing beside his house:
a watering can at hand, his eyes
to the ground.

The ground around him is damp;
his desire is fled and gone. What he
does not wish to know, under any
circumstances, is where and when he will be
demanded back and claimed
by the ground around him.

*

Its only riddle: *how*
it is; how that leaves it

at a loss, at less
than a loss, for words.

That I'm standing straight among rising plants.
That what encircles me like a world
takes possession of me, just as
what I keep veiled like a mist
wants to be possessed

by me. Listen! as the stone
splits the stream, so the chestnut keeps
its shiny silence; the antlion will never
embrace its ant and help it out of the funnel,
back to its antlike freedom.

*

Shortly before it is too late,
what was called beauty passes away

at least to the lightfall in the navel
of an old man, who, thinking he might

die, no longer took the trouble
to close his curtains. And yet

it remains the same river, which, delirious
with love, wishes, thinks, pierces, is.

Time and again I have to love you,
for you are what is so utterly strange
to me; almost as strange to me

as my being's core, which is
a wingbeat still lasting
long after the memory

of my name has evaporated. Sometimes,
once I become aware of myself
and our house starts to rustle
and I am tempted to call out

your name, I find you in my head
again, as if I had not meant
to caress you, caress you so.

As soon as I raise my eyes
the invisible has slipped away
and I begin to see what I see:
memories of what I have seen

and whatever I will see. By seeing
I keep remembering;

hoping that I exist.

Especially when I look at her
as she runs her hand like that
through her hair, her elbow
resting on her knee, and she
says something to me.

*

She has let herself fall on her bed
just as she fell there. But now she is
no longer crying; her makeup has run,
drying gold-dust stains her cheek,
her hair is dishevelled.

On the folding screen which has no
more chances to get used to her,
a dragon is forever diving for its pearl,
Zeno's arrow is followed time and again
by another which splits it in two.

*

Seldom has a panther's leap
anything at all of the same leap
by the same panther, unless as
willed by the panther itself.

The dolphin swimming in front of the ship
keeps swimming in front of the ship
until there is definitely no longer
a dolphin swimming in front of a ship.

And so it will come to pass that you scarcely notice

the sweat in your armpits changing smell,
that you fail to see the centaur scrape
his hooves before he advances towards you,
and here where you're safe at home
kicks and smashes it all to smithereens.

*

'Then they went away too.'
Hardly had I known them.
I also hardly stayed behind.
I would have liked to write something
down, but I had forgotten to write

it down. If you listen

to people, it's all about a future
which lives in a pebble and is as smooth
as the self-same pebble. Now and again
I own such a pebble as well: a moment
before I've thrown it away.

*

As simple as a drop of water,
as clear as a splinter of birch,

Because the foal falls patiently, cautiously
out of the horse and is able to stand,

And the fish unfolds like a metal tear
and is able to fly, and people quand même

Are slow to learn silence and absence
amidst their armored scree,

It isn't as simple, as clear
what I'm left with when I
have put down my pen.

JEROME ROTHENBERG

At Tsukiji Market Tokyo

I
fish & styrofoam
& plastic wrappings
where we watched great tuna bodies
white still under frost
on carts that pass us by
here in this market without smells
a place for noble death
for fish death
we can view it from our chariot
this flat bed
moving forward—curving—in a dream
small fishes packed in rows
a giant clam like a vagina
a razor-beak *sayori* red dot at its tip
the *kimme* showing god's large eye
(he said) or under lamplight
gills still moving
fish blood seeping out
the blood of white fish with what stolen beauty
orange fins & tails of poison *fugu*
nearby eels in vats of blood & water
& the dark saws splitting flesh & bone
the severed tuna heads their mouths still open
black fish wrapped in ice
a red slash underneath its head
eye wide & dry
a cavity that cuts down deep
that lets the hand move in & out
to draw out lungs & guts

shrimps wriggling   sad survivors   in the sawdust
"insects of the sea"
my mind aswim with these
with mouths that open in the blood they float through
miles of searching filaments
like flags for death
a paradise of bubbles fast ascending
tiny eggs & sperm
each one a seedbed for a hundred kannons
breaking into life
the cry of food & sex so strong
there is no wrapper can contain it
but it fills the air
& from my mouth it issues like the dead
the voices of our fathers calling
ploughed back in the earth
without regrets
reminding us how gorgeous death is
blood of fishes staining the white flesh
red flowers & round open eyes

2 THE TALE

He walks among the others: animals & neighbors. In the land of is-
lands someone comes to meet him, tall & with an eye that cuts
through space. Immaculate. The man cries out & falls. His death
comes when it does by force of nature. In this way we feel the earth
shake till it draws the light around us. Lungs and guts are emptied.
When the shock breaks through the crust a block of houses rises
from the sea and burrows down. Its people lie beneath a wall of
boulders: stones a god shakes free. They see the fish swept up into a
stranger's net. The corridors are white & lined with fish blood.
Death is always sudden, always comes after the fatal blow. A mallet
cracks the fish skull. They blast a hole into the fish's maw. The
messengers who spoke a broken language, also now stare through
broken eyes. We walk among the shelters & the empty lots. Awash

in Tsukiji where the boards cry out with fish death. Continue with the work he hands you. To provoke & probe. A life disrupted is no less a life. Those who were sleeping when the floats drove by continued sleeping. Those who were awake were faster—like fathers running in & out of dreams. The prince of tides has written this for you. The land of islands.

3
"a great quake
"shook the earth
the old poem has it
thinking how our legs have lost their balance
books & ladders tumbling down
a dream of fish death

where the bathers in their terror move like fish
the man who has an old world in his mind
sees it return to him
the year behind him lost to sleep
a rush of water dims his eyes
the words rewoven to the present day

.

[HOJOKI—CHOMEI AT TOYAMA—1212 A.D.—KOBE 1995/96]

months passed & people spoke about the quake no longer
but a skull would sometimes turn up in the earth
heavy with water
& the aftershocks now were inside us
carried with us day by day
the earthquake hidden underneath the ground
our houses like our ashes swept away

this is how a capital can disappear
or boats be swallowed by the earth
covered by mountains
a city with dead houses (someone thinks)
how long will they be standing?
—until the wild boars clog up all your streets
—until the mountain cleaves in two

days grow darker
world knows what its equal is
an earthquake spewing havoc all around us
when the elements light up
the days go white with aftershocks & black with clouds
houses slip into the earth consumed as dust
like that stirred up by horses racing through a valley
where land gives way & blights them
trapped in the event

but when they speak the language of the gods
no words come out
therefore the masks they use are hinged
to make a show of speech

no one is free of it   no heart
escapes its vanities
but all their things record the years that pass
the way the wind shadows their months
all times abandoned to its ceaseless shaking
like a dragon moving up & down
like thunderbolts that strike them dead
like smoke that covers a pagoda
waves that break on rocks
seas burying the earth

a fish
under the light

a message brought out of the shadows
fin & claw
& claw
tearing at your throat

periphery
pursuing

torn to shreds

how many years before it ends?
how dark the sin? how raw the talk that ends it?
how cruel the buddha who resides here
who abides catastrophes & fires
aftershocks of quakes that pass us by
events that raise us on their wings
then let us crash   pale billows
swelling up around the little temples
the little shorelines under water
rivers driven skyward in one final quake

.

forgotten with the dead
in glory
massive bodies hidden under frost

the words recorded
of a man beside himself who speaks
who says

"be here
"pretend

(so like the world they are
so like the man himself

the water underneath his window
still a haven for lost birds

uncertain thoughts
uncertain passage through a foreign world

Kazuko Shiraishi

translated from the Japanese by Samuel Grolmes
& Yumiko Tsumura

A Bear of the Human Family

The man was walking through the nursery
Oho!   we meet again
There is no greeting but   it is a face
He happens to see   once in a while   it is a bear
"We are not friends   but we make it a mutual
Rule not to violate each other's world"
The man   always walks empty-handed, carrying no weapon
But says he's not afraid   of course other employees
Carry spray guns
"The bear   senses my feelings instinctively"
Even though someone was attacked by a bear on a nearby golf
     course   and
Killed   the bear
One day   when a beaver came and gnawed down the important
     old cherry tree, too
He just said
"It came from a nearby river"
A family of seven or eight deer who are permanent residents
Badgers   and   and

And today too   the man walks   through the nursery
Slowly   slowly   with his enormous body
Looking at it
A bear has added a new line to the myths of Canada
Recently a bear of the human family appeared too
                              It's a good phenomenon

The Residents of the Cocoon

We   are not a chrysalis, but
Why   are we in a silkworm cocoon
We   even sprouted wings and can fly well enough, but
When we notice   we are in a cocoon

Strange, isn't it?   The other day we were flying in the sky, but
When we notice   it seems we are in a cocoon
Covered with   many   thin veils
Since we cannot see outside well
Without knowing how the world is   we eat and sleep
Our eyes   blurred
Ears   ambiguous   mouths useless
Since we don't use clear words or voices
I don't want to speak to you   anymore
Being told such things   we cannot even pretend to be friends
That's the kind of dream I had   last night

We   are not a chrysalis, but
Why   are we in a silkworm cocoon
Who made the cocoon who   shut us up
In a cocoon?   No   we
Forget language in a cocoon   forget the world
Forget even that we made the cocoon   by ourselves
Indifferent to the fact that our wings have degenerated (the insensitivity
    disease)
Even though we have wings we are just like a chrysalis
Even if the cocoon disappears we pretend we cannot fly
                           stay put   stay put

The Wild Pigs of Kalimantan

If there is one monkey   it plays one violin
But if a hundred monkeys   go on a spree   a hundred violins
  begin to squeak in the woods
This   is the jungle of Kalimantan
Taufik is a veterinarian   he says that
The wild pigs   are always afraid of the sight of human beings   in-
    stantly hide themselves   but   one day
Because of a spontaneous fire
The virgin forest with ample water   dense
Green from ancient times all at once broke into huge flames
Those wild pigs that are afraid of human beings   squealing
  come bounding this way   in unison   the soles of their feet
  badly burnt from stepping on grains of fire
The wild pigs!
The wild pigs!   how should we apologize
How   should we explain   the cruel acts   of the ugly human beings
  what kind of   punishment should come to them
  Once
There were red birds in Kalimantan
I have met   those birds   in Paris
On the streets with large luxuriant Benjamin trees in front of the old
    palace
Love was overflowing
From the throats of the red birds in lined up cages searching out
The passersby and pecking at their food

The wild pigs are walking this way   crashing through my notebook
    plunging their burnt black hooves of fire grains into my heart

From The Precious Tears of the Donkey

One day   I asked the donkey   where are
Your tears   she did not tell me
I went out   to Malacca
To meet the spirit of Malacca   but the moon shines
Fish and birds do not answer   sleep deeply
No one   knows where the spirit is
I too   sleep deeply
At dawn   a carpenter bird sings   Malacca   Malacca
If I were a tree, I would answer
Malacca's soul lives inside my seed
Because Malacca is the name of a tree
You don't have to know that
It doesn't necessarily have to be a tree
    Moon or   bird or fish would be fine
Malacca's sand   is wet with the tears   of a thin sea shell

The Donkey   Speculates

Should she call   or not
Even though she wants to call   the donkey   wonders
As if she had become a nation
The line might be tapped
It's dangerous   to leak information   and
She thinks of the cute   mountain girl Heidi
Surrounded by sheep   mountain sheep   running through the green
    fields
Heidi   of the sweet   lips
Isn't she   too unsuspicious   too innocent   passionate   tossing
An ideal ball   to this side of the telephone
The donkey   like a housewife knitting   speculates
On this and that adding stitches   changing stitches

The Afternoon of the Sheep

Yesterday   I met   a new
Animal   who is playing a game where things like the soul aren't needed
It has glass eyes   a computer in its chest
I can't see the tails and all   because of the shadows of the buildings

But   the lives of the sheep   don't change
They go to the hills   take off their clothes   and put on priests robes
Nowadays   even the gods   tend to take business trips
(No   even the gods   want to avoid the sheep
                                        in priests robes)
No one wants to be made a victim   but
To carry through one's own truth   justice is comfortable
At times like that   desires
Come along   tempting the executioners

Look   at the hills where the sheep   are buried
Even though they are buried   even though they are buried
The sheep   do not die
Even from inside sausages   they come back to life
The sheep spew out from the entire body
The fluff of the clouds of poesy
Sending the eternal executioners   over to the other side
In this way   for centuries   tens of centuries
In the afternoon   we   see   the hills where the spirits of
The sheep whose severed lives   were turned into total silence
Fly over in the sky   Oh   the hill of the sheep
                    That is   the hill of the sheep

The Seven Cats Are Happy

The seven cats   are happy
Always with the poet and his wife
East   to West
When they came from that side   to this side
They got shots from the doctor
They got visas and passports with names and IDs
They traveled safely

Whoever lives next door
The cats are happy
Always with the poet and his wife
Whoooo is the poet's mother
Wheeere is her grave
Why   did you decide to live on this side
You don't need to know why
The quiet poet   doesn't say anything
The sweet   wife   is a good cook

The seven cats   were happy   happy
Ten years have passed since then
They have gotten too old and three of them died last year
Three died last year
It can't be helped
Whoooo is the poet's mother
Wheeere is her grave
So   they have decided to live on this side
This   is a very fine place
The quiet poet speaks for the first time   a comment
My wife   is really
        a good cook

Tomas Tranströmer
translated from the Swedish by Robin Fulton

THE GREAT ENIGMA

Eagle Rock

Behind the vivarium glass
the reptiles
unmoving.

A woman hangs up washing
in the silence.
Death is becalmed.

In the depths of the ground
my soul glides
silent as a comet.

Facades

I
At road's end I see power
and it's like an onion
with overlapping faces
coming loose one by one . . .

II
The theatres are emptied. It's midnight.
Words blaze on the facades.
The enigma of the unanswered letters
sinks through the cold glitter.

November

When the hangman's bored he turns dangerous.
The burning sky rolls up.

Tapping sounds can be heard from cell to cell
and space streams up from the ground-frost.

A few stones shine like full moons.

Snow Is Falling

The funerals keep coming
more and more of them
like the traffic signs
as we approach a city.

Thousands of people gazing
in the land of long shadows.

A bridge builds itself
slowly
straight out in space.

Signatures

I have to step
over the dark threshold.
A hall.
The white document gleams.
With many shadows moving.
Everyone wants to sign it.

Until the light overtook me
and folded up time.

Haiku

I

With hanging gardens,
a lama monastery.
Painted battle scenes.

*

Wall of hopelessness . . .
The doves flutter to and fro.
They have no faces.

*

Thoughts standing still, like
the colored mosaic stones in
the palace courtyard.

*

On the balcony
I stand in a cage of sun-
beams—like a rainbow.

*

Humming in the mist.
A fishing-boat far from land
—trophy on the waves.

*

Glittering cities:
song, stories, mathematics—
but with a difference.

II

Stag in blazing sun.
The flies sew, sew, fasten that
shadow to the ground.

III

A chill-to-the-bone
wind flows through the house tonight—
names of the demons.

*

Gaunt tousled pine-trees
on the same tragic moorland.
Always and always.

*

Borne by the darkness.
I met an immense shadow
in a pair of eyes.

*

The November sun—
my enormous shadow swims
becomes a mirage.

*

Those milestones, always
on their way somewhere. Listen
—a stock-dove calling.

*

Death stoops over me.
I'm a problem in chess. He
has the solution.

IV

The sun disappears.
The tugboat looks on with its
face of a bulldog.

*

On a rocky ledge
the crack in the charmed cliff shows.
The dream an iceberg.

*

Working up the slopes
in open sunlight—the goats
that foraged on fire.

V

And blueweed, blueweed
keeps rising from the asphalt.
It's like a beggar.

*

The darkening leaves
in autumn are as precious
as the Dead Sea Scrolls.

VI

Sitting on a shelf
in the library of fools
the sermons untouched.

*

Come out of the swamp!
The sheatfish tremble with laughter
when the pine strikes twelve.

*

My happiness swelled
in those Pomeranian
swamps and the frogs sang.

*

He writes, writes and writes . . .
Glue floated in the canals.
On the Styx, that barge.

*

Go, quiet as a shower
and meet the whispering leaves.
Hear the Kremlin's bell!

VII

Perplexing forest
where God lives without money.
The walls were shining.

*

Encroaching shadows . . .
We are astray in the woods
in the mushroom clan.

*

Black-and-white magpie
stubbornly running zigzag
right across the fields.

*

See how I'm sitting
like a punt pulled up on land.
Here I am happy.

*

The avenues trot
in a harness of sunbeams.
Did someone call out?

VIII

The grass is rising—
his face is a runic stone
raised in memory.

*

Here's a dark picture.
Poverty painted-over,
flowers in prison dress.

IX

When the hour is here
the blind wind will come to rest
against the facades.

*

I've been in that place—
all over a white-washed wall
the flies crowd and crowd.

*

Here where the sun burned . . .
a mast holding a black sail
from long long ago.

*

Hold on, nightingale!
Out of the depths it's growing—
we are in disguise.

X

Death leans forward and
writes on the ocean surface.
While the church breathes gold.

*

Something has happened.
The moon filled the room with light.
God knew about it.

*

The roof broke apart
and the dead man can see me
can see me. That face.

*

Hear the swish of rain.
To reach right into it I
whisper a secret.

*

Station platform scene.
What unpredictable calm—
it's the inner voice.

XI

A revelation.
The long-standing apple-tree.
The sea is close-by.

*

The sea is a wall.
I can hear the gulls screaming—
they're waving at us.

*

God's wind in the back.
The shot that comes soundlessly—
a much-too-long dream.

*

Ash-colored silence.
The blue giant passes by.
Cool breeze from the sea.

*

A wind vast and slow
from the ocean's library.
Here's where I can rest.

*

Birds in human shape.
The apple-trees in blossom.
The great enigma.

Kamau Brathwaite

The Visibility Trigger

■

and so they came up over the reefs

up the creeks & rivers
oar prong put-put
hack tramp silence

and i was dreaming near morning

i offered you a kola nut
your fingers huge & smooth & red
and you took it your dress makola blue

and you broke it into gunfire

■

the metal was hot & jagged
it was as if the master of bronze
had poured anger into his cauldron

and let it spit spit sputter
and it was black spark green in my face
it was as if a maggot had slapped me in the belly

and i had gone soft like the kneed of my wife's bread

i could hear salt leaking out of the black hole of kaneshie
i could hear grass growing around the edges of the green lake

i could hear stalactites ringing in my cave of vision

bats batting my eyes shut
their own eyes howling like owls in the dead dark

and they marched into the village
and our five unready virginal elders met them

bowl calabash oil carafe of fire silence

and unprepared & venerable I was dreaming mighty wind in trees
our circles talismans round hut round village cooking pots

the world was round & we the spices in it
time wheeled around our memories like stars

yam cassava groundnut sweetpea bush
and then it was yams again

birth child hunter warrior
and the breath

that is no more

which is birth which is child which is hunter which is warrior
which is breath

that is no more

■

and they brought sticks rods roads bullets straight objects
birth was not breath

but gaping wound

hunter was not animal
but market sale

warrior was child
that is no more

and i beheld the cotton tree
guardian of graves rise upward from its monument of
grass

■

crying aloud in its vertical hull
calling for crashes of branches vibrations of leaves

there was a lull of silver

■

and then the great grandfather gnashing upwards from its teeth
of roots. split down its central thunder

the stripped violated wood crying aloud its murder. the leaves'
frontier signals alive with lamentations

and our great odoum
triggered at last by the ancestors into your visibility

crashed
into history

How Europe Underdeveloped Africa

to be blown into fragments. your flesh
like the islands that you loved
like the seawall that you wished to heal

bringing equal rights & justice to the brothers
a fearless cumfa mashramani to the sisters whispering their
free/zon
that grandee nanny's histories be listened to with all their ancient

flèches of respect

until they are the steps up the poor of the church
up from the floor of the hill/slide
until they become the roar of the nation

that fathers would at last settle into what they own
axe adze if not oil well. torch
light of mackenzie

that those who have all these generations
bitten us bare to the bone
gnawing our knuckles to their stone

price fix price rise rachman & rat/chet squeeze
how bread is hard to buy how rice is scarcer than the
muddy water where it rides

how bonny baby bellies grow doom-laden dungeon grounded down
to groaning in their hunger
grow wailer voiced & red eyed in their anger

that knocks against their xylophones of prison ribs
that how we cannot give our wives or sleephearts or our children
or our children's children a sweetend trip to kenya. watch

maasai signal from their saffron shadow
the waterbuck & giraffe wheel round wrecked manyatta
while little blonder kinter

who don't really give a fart
for whom this is the one more yard
a flim. for whom this is the one/off start

to colon cortez cecil rhodes
for whom this is the one more road
to the soff-voiced thathi-headed waiter

aban. died out of his shit by his baas. at the nairobi airport hotel

but lets his face sulk into i soup
lets his hairshirt wrackle i sweat
cause i man am wearing the tam of his dream in i head

that these & those who fly still dread/er up the sky
vultures & hawks. eye
scarpering morgan the mi/ami mogol

those night beast a babylon who heiss us on sus

but that worse it is the blink
in iani own eye. the sun blott. ed out by
paper a cane fires vamp.

ires a ink wheels emp.
ires a status quo status quo status crows
that tell a blood tale toll/ing in the ghetto

till these small miss/demeanours as you call them
be
come a monstrous fetter on the land that will not let us breed

un. til every chuse in the face of good morning
be
come one more coil one more spring one more no

thing to sing/about
be
come the boulder rising in the bleed

the shoulder nourishing the gun
the headlines screaming of the skrawl across the wall
of surbiton of trenton town of sheraton hotel

dat **POR CYAAAN TEK NO MOOR**

& the babies & their mothers & their mothers & their
mothers mothers & their mothers mothers mothers mothers
sizzled forever in the semi-automatic catcalls of the orange heat

flare up of siren. howl of the scorch wind wail
through the rat-tat-rat-a-tat-tat
of the hool through the tap of your head. damp. stench. criall

the well of war flame drilling through your flesh

reduced to the time before green/bone
reduced to the time before ash/skull
reduced to the time before love/was born

in your arms
before dawn was torn from your pillow
in your arms

before the tumours were crumpled into paper bags
inside the star/broek market

in your arms

before the knife ran through the dark & locket steel
between the spine & kidney

in your arms
in your arms
in your arms

i prophesay

before you recognized the gorgon head inside the red eye
of the walkie talkie

■

to be blown into fragments. your death
like the islands that you loved
like the seawall that you wished to heal

bringing equal rights & justice to the bredren
that the children above all others would be like the sun.
rise

over the rupununi over the hazy morne de castries over kilimanjaro

any where or word where there is love there is the sky & its blue
free
where past means present struggle

towards vlissengens where it may some day end

distant like powis on the essequibo
drifting like miracles or dream
or like that lonely fishing engine slowly losing us its sound

but real like your wrist with its tick of blood around its man.
acles of bone
but real like the long marches the court steps of tryall

the sudden sodden night journeys up the pomeroon
holed up in a different safe house every morning & try
ing to guess from the heat of the hand.

shake if the stranger was stranger or cobra or friend
& the urgent steel of the kis.
kadee glittering its *qqurl* down the steepest bend in the breeze

& the leaves

ticking & learning to live with the smell of rum on the skull's
breath. his cigarette ash on the smudge of your fingers
his footsteps into your houses

& having to say it over & over & over again
with your soft ringing patience with your black.
lash of wit. though the edges must have been curling with pain

but the certainty clearer & clearer & clearer again

that it must be too simple to hit/too hurt
not to remember

that it must not become an easy slogan or target
too torn too defaced too devalued down in redemption market

that when men gather govern other manner

they should be honest in a world of hornets

that bleed into their heads like lice
corruption that cockroaches like a dirty kitchen sink

that politics should be like understanding of the floor.
boards of your house

swept clean each morning. built by hands that know
the wind & tide & language

from the loops within the ridges of the koker
to the rusty tinnin fences of your yard

so that each man on his cramped restless island
on backdam of his land in forest clearing by the broeken river
where berbice struggles against slushy ground

takes up his bed & walks

in the power & the reggae of his soul/stice
from the crippled brambled pathways of his vision
to the certain limpen knowledge of his nam

■

this is the message that the dreadren will deliver
groundation of the soul with drift of mustard seed

that when he spoke the world was fluter on his breeze
since it was natural to him like the water. like the way he listened

like the way he walked. one a dem ital brothers who had grace

for being all these things & careful of it too

& careless of it too
he was cut down plantation cane

because he dared to grow & growing/green
because be was that slender reed & there were machetes sharp
enough to hasten him & bleed

be was blown down

because his bridge from man to men
meant doom to prisons of a world we never made
meant wracking out the weeds that kill our yampe vine

∎

& so the bomb
fragmenting islands like the land you loved

letting back darkness in

∎

but there are stars that burn that murders do not know
soft diamonds behind the blown to bits

that trackers will not find that bombers will not see
that scavengers will never hide away

∎

the caribbean bleeds near georgetown prison

∎

a widow rushes out & hauls her children free

Stone

for Mikey Smith 1954–1983
Stoned to death on Stony Hill, Kingston

When the stone fall that morning out of the johncrow sky

it was not dark at first . that opening on to the red sea humming
but something in my mouth like feathers . blue like bubbles
carrying signals & planets & the sliding curve of the
world like a water pic. ture in a raindrop when the pressure. drop

When the stone fall that morning out of the johncrow sky

i couldn't cry out because my mouth was full of beast & plunder
as if i was gnashing badwords among tombstones
as if that road up stony hill. round the bend by the church
yard . on the way to the post office . was a bad bad dream

& the dream was like a snarl of broken copper wire zig zagg.
ing its electric flashes up the hill & splitt. ing spark & flow.
ers high. er up the hill . past the white houses & the ogogs bark.
ing all teeth & fur. nace & my mother like she up . like she up.

like she up. side down up a tree like she was scream.
like she was scream. like she was scream. in no & no.
body i could hear could hear a word i say . in . even though
there were so many poems left & the tape was switched on &

runn. in & runn. in &
the green light was red & they was stannin up there &
evva. where in london & amsterdam & at unesco in paris &
in west berlin & clapp. in & clapp. in & clapp. in &

not a soul on stony hill to even say amen

Kamau Brathwaite   213

■

& yet it was happenin happenin happenin

the fences begin to crack in i skull .
& there was a loud boodoooooooooooooooooooooooongs like
guns going off . them ole time magnums .

or like a fireworks a dreadlocks was on fire .
& the gaps where the river comin down
inna the drei gully where my teeth use to be smilin .
& i tuff gong tongue that use to press against them & parade

pronunciation . now unannounce & like a black wick in i head &
dead .
& it was like a heavy heavy riddim bow down in i belly . bleedin dub
& there was like this heavy heavy black dog thump. in in i chest &

pump. in

murderrrrrrrrrrrrrrrrrrrrrrrrrrrrrrrrrrrrrrrrrrrrrrrrrrrrrrrr

& i throat like dem tie. like dem tie. like dem tie a tight tie a.
round it. twist. in my name quick crick . quick crick .
& a nevva wear neck. tie yet .

& a hear when de big boot kick down i door . stump
in it foot pun a knot in de floor. board .
a window slam shat at de back a mi heart .

de itch & oooze & damp a de yaaad
in my silver tam. bourines closer & closer .
st joseph marching bands crash. in & closer . &

bom si. cai si. ca boom ship bell . bom si. cai si. ca boom ship bell

& a laughin more blood & spittin out
lawwwwwwwwwwwwwwwwwwwwwwwwwwwwwwwwwwwwwwwd

i two eye lock to the sun & the two sun starin back black
from de grass

& a bline to de butterfly fly. in

■

& it was like a wave on stony hill caught in a crust of sun.
light

■

& it was like a matchstick schooner into harbour muffled in the
silence of it wound

■

& it was like the blue of speace was filling up the heavens
wid its thunder

& it was like the wind was grow. in skin. the skin had hard hairs
harderin

■

it was like marcus garvey rising from his coin .
stepping towards his people crying dark

& every mighty word be trod. the ground fall dark & hole
be. hine him like it was a bloom x. ploding sound .

my ears was bleed. in sound

■

& i was quiet now because i had become that sound

the sun. light morning washed the choral limestone harsh
against the soft volcanic ash. i was

& i was slippin past me into water. & i was slippin past me
into root. i was

& i was
slippin past me into flower. & i was rippin upwards

into shoot. i was

& every politrician tongue in town was lash.
ing me with spit & cut. rass wit & ivy whip & wrinkle jumbimum

it was like warthog . grunt. in in the ground

& children running down the hill run right on through the splash
of pouis that my breathe. ing make when it was howl & red &

bubble

& sparrow twits pluck tic & tap. worm from the grass
as if i man did nevva have no face. as if i man did never in this

place

■

When the stone fall that morning out of the johncrow sky

i could not hold it brack or black it back or block it off or limp
away or roll it from me into memory or light or rock it steady into
night. be

cause it builds me now with leaf & spiderweb & soft & crunch &
like the pow.
derwhite & slip & grit inside your leather. boot &
fills my blood with deaf my bone with hobbledumb & echo.
less neglect neglect neglect neglect &

lawwwwwwwwwwwwwwwwwwwwwwwwwwwwwwwwwwwwwwwww

∎

i am the stone that kills me

Charles Tomlinson

Song

To enter the real,
how far
must we feel beyond
the world in which we already are?

It is all here
but we are not. If we could see
and hear only half
the flawed symphony,

we might cease
nervously to infer
the intentions of
an unimaginable author

and stand,
senses and tongues unbound,
in the spaces of that land
our fathers brought us to,

where, what will be well
or not well,
only time
or time's undoing can tell.

Second Song

On each receding bush,
the stipple of snow today
has posted into the distance
this silent company

on the alert for openings
which yesterday were not there,
tracking through field and covert
into the fullness here;

and not on bushes only,
but on stump, root, stone—
why is it a change of weather merely
finds directions where there were none?—

so that each Roman road,
on entering the maze,
crosses the hills in confusion
at the infinity of ways

only a little snow
has chalked in everywhere,
as if a whole landscape might be unrolled
out of the atmosphere.

Zipangu

1 THE PINES AT HAKONE

The pine trees will not converse with foreigners. Their aim
is to hide everything that lies beneath their crisp, dense foliage
or at their feet—those ferns, for instance, that reproduce
the pine pattern on every leaf and lie low
the air scarcely stirring them. They have learned
to keep secrets by studying the tall trunks that surround them
and that might still be living in the Edo period.
Touched by the breeze, they rock on their pliant roots
and shift slightly their green vestments, beginning to oscillate,
to lean from side to side, even to bow—
though not deeply as is customary with this people—,
as if good manners were all they had on their minds
and they had spent a long time considering the question
without coming to any conclusion. The tiny agitations of the wood
are on the surface only, and they soon resolve themselves
into the general unison of branches, heaving, subsiding.
Today the clouds are as secretive as those branches
and they refuse to reveal the summit or the sides
of Fujiyama. You sense it there, but you cannot see
its bulk or its snow-streaks that Japanese art
has made so famous. (Hiroshige was here
but on a clearer morning.) Days later
and back in the capital, I watch the carp
in the pond of the Yasukuni shrine. These fish
in their extrovert muscularity, their passion for food
are all the trees are not; they steer themselves unerringly
with a blunt muscular force, their whiskered circular mouths
forming the o which means *give*, rolling over
on one another's backs, to get what is given, and arriving
with the massive bodily impetus
of legless sumo wrestlers ruddered by flickering tails.
But this is a military shrine, its gate a tall ideogram

topped by a bar like a gigantic gun-barrel
and the mere good manners of trees do not serve here
to distract the visitor from what he wishes to understand.
Though when he rises to go, the lit lanterns,
as if disguise were after all the mark of this nation,
throw through the branches a light of festivity, a carnival glow,
their object solely to beautify the spot
and make us forget what stern ghosts linger here.

2 HERON

The river crosses the city over a series of falls:
at each of the falls, waiting for fish
a small white heron—sometimes
a whole group of them, all
at a respectful distance from one another.
Perhaps they have fished the river too long—
they seldom visibly produce anything from it.
Perhaps their decorative tininess is the result
merely of malnutrition. They are indifferent to traffic
flowing by on either side, and to strollers
who pause to see what they might catch.
They watch the water with such an exemplary patience,
they seem to be leftovers from a time
when the world was filled with moral admonitions
and everything had been put there to mean something.
We, however, fail to take the lesson to heart
and continue to worry over their inadequate diet.
As evening arrives, the light on the buildings
goes golden, an Italian light, and the mountains
darken and press forward to stand protectively
round the city. Midnight
and below the roadway, in the glare of passing cars,
huddle the heron, roosting with one leg raised, and bent
even in sleep, towards the flash, the fish, the disappointment.

3 Shugakuin Garden

The variegated tremor
of the reflected foliage
brings autumn to the ponds:

the rising fish
create circles within circles,
pools within pools:

under garden branches
there is every sort of water
to be seen and listened to

as it talks its way downhill
through the leat of its channel
out into the rice beyond:

you will find no frontier
between the garden and the field,
between utility and beauty here.

4 Yamadera

You go by the local line:
schoolchildren keep getting off the train,
returning to those villages
beneath vertical mountains.
Kumagane: conical hills
beyond the little station;
Sakunami: the sky is darkening
and so are the trees;
it will rain soon—in time
for our arrival
by this narrow way
to the deep north,

though 'deep,' they say,
is a mistranslation
of the title of Bashō's book,
and 'far' would be more accurate,
'though less poetic,' they add.
The river in the ravine,
this intimate progress between sheer slopes,
what must it have been
for a traveller
on foot and horse-back?
Our rail-track way
is a smooth ascent
through turning maples
into cooling autumn air,
the faint aroma of snow in it.
It was here he wrote—
but would not write today—
the shriek of the cicada
penetrates
the heart of the rock.
He came, then, in heat.
The climb up the mountain face
which is the temple
must have cost him sweat,
his feet on the thousand steps
that lead past the door of each shrine
up to the look-out where
you can take in the entire valley,
echoing, this afternoon,
with shot on shot
from a whole army
of automatic scarecrows.
The rain arrives, but does not stay,
from a grey cloud
darkening half the sky

and disappearing. On the way down
we see once again
what arrested our upward climb—
stones to the miscarried,
and prayer-wheels
to wish the unborn
a reincarnation in a human form.
And so we depart
in the light that saw his arrival—
that of late afternoon,
to wait for the train
in this still distant corner. Clearly
the poetry of 'deep'
is more accurate
than mere accuracy—
a journey to the interior
is what it must have felt like then.
They say he came as a spy
(the villages are passing in reverse order now),
that there was more to it than met the eye,
calling on abbots and warriors,
to sniff out plots before they occurred.
There is no doubt, some say,
others that it is absurd
to speculate now. And so
we leave Bashō to disappear,
deeper and deeper,
while we cross the angular paddies
towards the shapeless cities,
the mountains already drawing apart
on either side of the wide plain
into two great parallels
echoing the track of our train,
our own narrow way south.

5 EPILOGUE

This advanced frontier
of Asia, this chain
of volcanoes, arcadian,
alpine, weird,
its ravines noisy with waterfalls,
its countless rivers
too impetuous for navigation,
ports few and coast foam-fringed—
the tree-fern, bamboo,
banana and palm grow here
side by side
with pine, oak, beech and conifer.
Wild animals are not numerous
and no true wolf exists
(the domestic dog
is wolf-like but ill-conditioned).
The lobster stands for longevity
and all history before 500
must be classed as legendary.
This is the place
Marco Polo never visited
but, jailed by the Genovese,
rehearsed its wonders
in bad French
to a Pisan fellow prisoner
calling it
Zipangu.

Robert Creeley

Edges

Expectably slowed yet unthinking
of outside when in, or weather
as ever more than there when
everything, anything, will be again

Particular, located, familiar in its presence
and reassuring. The end
of the seeming dream was simply
a walk down from the house through the field.

I had entered the edges, static,
had been walking without attention,
thinking of what I had seen, whatever,
a flotsam of recollections, passive reflection.

My own battered body, clamorous
to roll in the grass, sky looming,
the myriad smells ecstatic, felt insistent prick of things
under its weight, wanted something

Beyond the easy, commodious adjustment
to determining thought, the loss of reasons
to ever do otherwise than comply—
tedious, destructive interiors of mind

As whatever came in to be seen,
representative, inexorably chosen,
then left as some judgment.
Here thought had its plan.

Is it only in dreams
can begin the somnambulistic rapture?
Without apparent eyes?
Just simply looking?

All these things were out there
waiting, innumerable, patient.
How could I name even one enough,
call it only a flower or a distance?

If ever, just one moment, a place
I could be in where all imagination would fade
to a center, wondrous, beyond any way
one had come there, any sense,

And the far-off edges of usual
place were inside. Not even the shimmering
reflections, not one even transient ring
come into a thoughtless mind.

Would it be wrong to say, *the sky is up,*
the ground is down, and out there
is what can never be the same—
what, like music, has gone?

Trees stay outside one's thought.
The water stays stable in its shifting.
The road from here to there continues.
One is included.

Here it all is then—
as if expected,
waited for and found
again.

Life & Death

"IF I HAD THOUGHT . . ."

If I had thought
one moment
to reorganize life
as a particular pattern,
to outwit distance, depth,
felt dark was myself
and looked for the hand
held out to me, I
presumed. It grew by itself.

•

It had seemed diligence,
a kind of determined
sincerity, just to keep going,
mattered, people would care
you were there.
I hadn't thought of death—
or anything that happened
simply because it happened.
There was no reason there.

"OH MY GOD . . ."

Oh my god—You
are a funny face
and your smile
thoughtful, your teeth
sharp—The agonies
of simple existence
lifted me up. But
the mirror I looked in
now looks back.

●

It wasn't God
but something else
was at the end,
I thought, would
get you like
my grandpa dead
in coffin
was gone forever,
so they said.

"OUT HERE . . ."

Out here there
is a soundless float
and the earth
seems far below—
or out. The stars
and the planets
glow on the wall.
Inside each one
we fuck, we fuck.

•

But I didn't mean to,
I didn't dare to look.
The first time couldn't
even find the hole
it was supposed to go in—
Lonely down here
in simple skin,
lonely, lonely
without you.

Sear at the center,
convoluted, tough passage,
history's knots,
the solid earth—
What streaked
consciousness, faint
design so secured
semen's spasm,
made *them*?

•

I didn't know then,
had only an avarice
to tear open
love and eat its person,
feeling confusion,
driven, wanting
inclusion, hunger
to feel, smell, taste
her flesh.

"IN THE DIAMOND . . ."

In the diamond
above earth,
over the vast, inchoate,
boiling *material*
plunging up, cresting
as a forming cup, on the truncated
legs of a man stretched out,
the nub of penis alert,
once again the story's told.

•

Born very young into a world
already very old, Zukofsky'd said.
I heard the jokes
the men told
down by the river, swimming.
What are you
supposed to do
and how do you learn.
I feel the same way now.

"THE LONG ROAD . . ."

The long road of it all
is an echo,
a sound like an image
expanding, frames growing
one after one in ascending
or descending order, all
of us a rising, falling
thought, an explosion
of emptiness soon forgotten.

●

As a kid I wondered
where do they go,
my father dead. The place
had a faded dustiness
despite the woods and all.
We all grew up.
I see our faces
in old school pictures.
Where are we now?

"WHEN IT COMES . . ."

When it comes,
it loses edge,
has nothing around it,
no place now present
but impulse not one's own,
and so empties into a river
which will flow on
into a white cloud
and be gone.

                •

Not me's going!
I'll hang on till
last wisp of mind's
an echo, face shreds
and moldering hands,
and all of whatever
it was can't say
any more to
anyone.

The Way

Somewhere in all the time that's passed
was a thing in mind became the evidence,
the pleasure even in fact of being lost
so quickly, simply that what it was could never last.

Only knowing was measure of what one could
make hold together for that moment's recognition,
or else the world washed over like a flood
of meager useless truths, of hostile incoherence.

Too late to know that knowing was its own reward
and that wisdom had at best a transient credit.
Whatever one did or didn't do was what one could.
Better at last believe than think to question?

There wasn't choice if one had seen the light,
not of belief but of that soft, blue-glowing fusion
seemed to appear or disappear with thought,
a minute magnesium flash, a firefly's illusion.

Best wonder at mind and let that flickering ambience
of wondering be the determining way you follow,
which leads itself from day to day into tomorrow,
finds all it ever finds is there by chance.

Nicanor Parra

translated from the Spanish by Liz Werner

Seven Voluntary Labors and One Seditious Act

1

the poet tosses stones into the lake
concentric circles multiply outward

2

the poet hoists himself up on a chair
to wind a clock that's hanging from the wall

3

the lyric poet gets down on his knees
in front of a blossoming cherry tree
and begins to recite the Lord's Prayer

4

the poet dresses up as a frogman
and kerplunks into the pool in the park

5

dangling from an umbrella
the poet hurls himself into the void
from the top floor of the Diego Portales Tower

6

the poet barricades himself in the Tomb of the Unknown Soldier
and from his post shoots poison arrows at the passers-by

7

the damned poet
amuses himself by throwing birds at stones

Seditious Act

the poet slits his wrists
in homage to the country of his birth

Something Like That

PARRA LAUGHS like he's condemned to hell
but when haven't poets laughed?
at least he declares that he's laughing

they pass the years pass
the years
at least they seem to be passing
hypothesis non fingo
everything goes on as if they were passing

now he starts to cry
forgetting that he's an antipoet

o

STOP RACKING YOUR BRAINS
nobody reads poetry nowadays
it doesn't matter if it's good or bad

o

FOUR DEFECTS that my Ophelia won't forgive me for:
old
lowlife
communist
and National Literature Prize

"My family may be able to forgive you
 for the first three
 but never for the last"

o

MY CORPSE and I
understand each other marvelously
my corpse asks me: do you believe in God?
and I respond with a hearty NO
my corpse asks: do you believe in the government?
and I respond with the hammer and sickle
my corpse asks: do you believe in the police?
and I respond with a punch in the face
then he gets up out of his coffin
and we go arm in arm to the altar

o

THE TRUE PROBLEM of philosophy
is who does the dishes

nothing otherworldly

God
      the truth
                the passage of time
absolutely
but first, who does the dishes

whoever wants to do them, go ahead
see ya later, alligator
                  and we're right back to being enemies

o

HOMEWORK ASSIGNMENT
compose a sonnet
                that begins with the following iambic pentameter line:
                I would prefer to die ahead of you
and that ends with the following:
                I would prefer that you be first to die

o

YOU KNOW what happened
while I was kneeling
in front of the cross
                looking at His wounds?

He smiled at me and winked!

before I thought He didn't ever laugh:
but now—yeah—I believe for real

o

A DECREPIT old man
throws red carnations
at his beloved mother's coffin

what you are hearing, ladies and gentlemen:
an old wino
bombarding his mother's tomb
with ribbons of red carnations

o

I QUIT sports for religion
(I went to mass every Sunday)
I abandoned religion for art
art for the mathematical sciences

until at last illumination hit

and now I'm someone only passing through
who puts no faith in the whole or its parts

To Make a Long Story Short

To make a long story short
I leave all of my possessions
to the Municipal Slaughterhouse
to the Special Forces Unit of the Police Department
to Lucky Dog Lotto

So now if you want you can shoot

A Resounding Zero

It all came down to nothing
& of the nothing, there is very little left

Note on the Lessons of Antipoetry

1.
In antipoetry, it is poetry that is sought, not eloquence.

2.
Antipoems should be read in the same order in which they were written.

3.
We must read poems with the same hunger we bring to antipoems.

4.
Poetry happens—so does antipoetry.

5.
The poet speaks to all of us, without discrimination.

6.
Often our pleasure in antipoetry is impaired by our curiosity: we attempt to understand and dispute when we shouldn't do either.

7.
Read in good faith if you want to partake, and don't ever find your satisfaction in the author's name.

8.
Ask your questions openly and listen without argument to the poets' words; don't be impatient with the pronouncements of the elders—they don't make them by accident.

9.
Hi to everyone.

HOMERO ARIDJIS

A Mexican born in 1940 in a village in the state of Morelia, Aridjis is a poet, novelist, former diplomat, and active environmentalist. New Directions published his *Eyes to See Otherwise: Selected Poems* in 2001. Other books in English translation include two earlier books of poetry, *Blue Spaces* (edited by Kenneth Rexroth) and *Exaltation of Light*; and the novels *1492: The Life and Times of Juan Cabezon of Castile*; *Persephone*; and *The Lord of the Last Days: Visions of the Year 1000*. He is the founder of the Group of 100, which promotes ecological awareness in Mexico.

The translator GEORGE McWHIRTER is an Irish poet long residing in Canada. He is the editor of the *Selected Poems of José Emilio Pacheco* and an anthology of Mexican poetry, *Where Words Like Monarchs Fly*. His books of poems include *Incubus: The Dark Side of the Light* and *A Staircase for All Souls*.

GENNADY AYGI

A Chuvash poet born in a village of the Chuvash Autonomous Republic of the Soviet Union in 1934, Aygi was persuaded by Boris Pasternak and Nazim Hikmet to write in Russian; he translated, however, a great deal of international poetry into his native language. Although internationally renowned, his books were not allowed to appear in the Soviet Union until the late 1980s. As a modernist folklorist, he has been said to be completely outside the Russian classical tradition, from Pushkin to Brodsky. New Directions published *Child-And-Rose* in 2003; *Field-Russia* is forthcoming. Three other books are available in English: *Selected Poems 1954–94*; *Salute—to Singing*; and *An Anthology of Chuvash Poetry*, which he edited.

The translator PETER FRANCE is the author of *Politeness and its Discontents*, and the editor of *The New Oxford Companion to Literature in French*; *The Oxford Guide to Literature in English Translation*; and *The Oxford History of Literary Translation in English*.

Bei Dao

A Chinese poet born in Beijing in 1949, Bei Dao was a co-founder in the 1970s of China's first samisdat magazine, *Jintian* (*Today*), which published the poets who were dismissed by literary critics as "Obscure" or "Misty." The name became attached to the group and, condemned by the government in the Anti-Spiritual Pollution Campaign, their work served as a poetic conscience for the Democracy Wall movement, and later for the students in Tiananmen Square. In exile since 1989, Bei Dao has lived in northern Europe and, for the last decade, in the US; his work is still largely banned in China. New Directions has published collections of short stories, *Waves* (1990); of essays, *Midnight's Gate* (2005); and of poetry: *The August Sleepwalker* (1990); *Old Snow* (1991); *Forms of Distance* (1994); *Landscape Over Zero* (1996); *Unlock* (2000); and *At the Sky's Edge: Poems 1991–1996* (2001). Also available in English translation is a book of essays, *The Blue House. Jintian* continues as the primary literary journal of the Chinese diaspora.

The co-translator Iona Man-Cheong is the author of *The Class of 1761: Examinations, State, and Elites in Late Imperial China*. "Ramallah" and "The Rose of Time" were translated by Bei Dao and Eliot Weinberger.

Kamau Brathwaite

A Barbadoan born in 1930, Brathwaite is a dramatist, cultural theorist, and the primary avant-gardist poet of the Anglophone Caribbean. He serves on the board of directors of UNESCO's History of Mankind project and as a cultural advisor to the government of Barbados. New Directions has published *Middle Passages* (1993); *Black + Blues* (1995); and *Ancestors* (2001), a complete reworking of his second epic trilogy on the African diaspora. *DS (2)* is forthcoming. Among his many other books of poetry are his first trilogy, *The Arrivants* (*Rights of Passage, Masks, Islands*); *Barabjan Poems 1492–1992*; and *Born to Slow Horses*. His books of prose include *The Development of Creole Society in Jamaica 1770–1820*; *History of the Voice: The Development of Nation Language in Anglophone Caribbean Poetry*; *Roots: Essays on Caribbean Literature*; and *The Zea*

Mexican Diary. Conversations with Nathaniel Mackey is a book-length interview.

ANNE CARSON

A Canadian born in Toronto in 1950, Carson is a poet and classicist. New Directions published her first book of poetry, *Glass, Irony, and God*, in 1995. Later books of poetry and other writings are *Plainwater*; *Autobiography of Red*; *The Beauty of the Husband*; *Men in the Off Hours*; and *Decreation*. Her criticism includes *Eros the Bittersweet* and *Economy of the Unlost* (*Reading Simonides of Keos with Paul Celan*). She is the translator of Sophocles' *Electra* and *If Not, Winter: Fragments of Sappho*.

INGER CHRISTENSEN

A Danish poet born in 1935, Christensen has become one of the best-known writers in Europe for the six books of poetry she has written in the last forty years. Most of her work is in long sequences and is written according to complicated rules of her own invention. *alphabet*, excerpted here, besides being abecedarian, is based on Fibonacci's mathematical sequence, in which each number is the sum of the previous two numbers. New Directions has published *alphabet* (2001) and *Butterfly Valley: A Requiem* (2004); the long book-length poem *It*, which many consider her masterwork, and her novel, *Azorno*, are forthcoming.

The translator SUSANNA NIED has translated Søren Ulrik Thomsen's *Selected Poems*, as well as all the poetry books of Inger Christensen.

ROBERT CREELEY

An American born in Massachusetts in 1926, Creeley was the author or editor of nearly a hundred books of poetry, fiction, correspondence, and critical prose. Beginning with his editorship of the *Black Mountain Review* in the 1950s, he was a central presence in U.S. poetry for five decades. New Directions published *Hello*

(1978); *Later* (1979); *Mirrors* (1983); *Memory Gardens* (1986); *Windows* (1990); *Echoes* (1994); *So There: Poems 1976–1983* (1998); *Life & Death* (1998); *Just in Time: Poems 1984–1994* (2001); and *If I Were Writing This* (2003); as well as his editions of Charles Olson's *Selected Writings* (1966) and George Oppen's *Selected Poems* (2003), and a collection of critical essays, edited by Tom Clark, *Robert Creeley and the Genius of the American Common Place* (1993). Other books include: *Collected Poems 1945–1975*; *Selected Poems*; *Collected Essays*; and *Collected Prose*. Robert Creeley died in 2005.

HANS FAVEREY

A Dutch poet born in Surinam (then Dutch Guiana) in 1933, Faverey spent most of his life in Holland and on the seacoast of Croatia. A clinical psychologist, he played and composed for the harpsichord, and had a particular attachment to the pre-Socratic philosophers. He wrote nine short books of crystalline lyrics. New Directions published *Against the Forgetting: Selected Poems* in 2004. Hans Faverey died in 1990.

The translator FRANCIS R. JONES has translated books of poetry from Bosnian-Croatian-Serbian (Vasko Popa, Mak Dizdar, Ivan Lalić), Hungarian (Miklós Radnóti), and Russian (Vyachleslav Kupriyanov), as well as many works by Dutch, Flemish, and Dutch-based Creole poets for anthologies and magazines.

FORREST GANDER

An American born in 1956, Gander grew up in Virginia and studied to be a geologist. New Directions has published his recent books of poetry: *Science & Steepleflower* (1998); *Torn Awake* (2001); and *Eye to Eye* (2005). Earlier poetry books include *Rush to the Lake*; *Lynchburg*; and *Deeds of Utmost Kindness*. His essays are collected in *A Faithful Existence: Reading, Memory, and Transcendence*. He is the translator of *No Shelter* by Pura López Colomé; *Mouth to Mouth: Poems by Twelve Contemporary Mexican Women*; a forthcoming selection of the poetry of Coral Bracho; and, with Kent Johnson, of *The Night* and *Immanent Visitor* by Jaime Saenz.

Gu Cheng

A Chinese poet born in 1956, Gu Cheng as a child was sent into internal exile during the Cultural Revolution. The youngest member of the *Today* group [see Bei Dao, above] and the most eccentric, his work moved from intense personal lyricism to long sequences that may well be the most radical poems written in Chinese. In exile on a small island in New Zealand, he tried to live as a Taoist sage. New Directions published *Sea of Dreams: Selected Writings* in 2005. Other books in English translation include an early *Selected Poems*; *Nameless Flowers*; and his strange roman-à-clef, *Ying'er*. In 1993, Gu Cheng committed suicide after murdering his wife.

The translator JOSEPH R. ALLEN is the author of *In the Voice of Others: Chinese Music Bureau Poetry* and the editor and additional translator of a new edition of Arthur Waley's version of *The Book of Songs*.

Susan Howe

An American poet born in 1937, Howe is the primary practitioner of the "poem with history," in the tradition of Pound and Olson. New Directions has published nearly all her poetry: *The Europe of Trusts* (1990); *The Non-Conformist's Memorial* (1993); *Frame Structures: Early Poems 1974–1979* (1996); *Pierce-Arrow* (1999); and *The Midnight* (2003). Her books of prose are the seminal *My Emily Dickinson* and *The Birth-mark: unsettling the wilderness in American literary history.*

Luljeta Lleshanaku

An Albanian poet born in 1968, Lleshanaku grew up under a form of house arrest and was not allowed to publish or attend university until the fall of the Enver Hoxha dictatorship in 1991. In a language that has only been written for less than a hundred years, Lleshanaku and the novelist Ismail Kadare are the first Albanian writers to achieve international recognition. New Directions published her *Fresco* in 2002. She works as a journalist in Tirana.

The translator HENRY ISRAELI is the author of a book of poetry,

New Messiahs. The poems here were co-translated with Ukzenel Buçpapa, Shpresa Qatapi, and Qazim Sheme.

NATHANIEL MACKEY

An American born in 1948 and a life-long resident of California, Mackey has been working for many years on two projects: the epistolary prose fiction, *From a Broken Bottle Traces of Perfume Still Emanate*, the first three volumes of which are *Bedouin Hornbook*, *Djbot Baghostus's Run*, and *Atet A.D.*; and the long poem, "Song of the Andoumboulou," which has appeared in *Eroding Witness, School of Udhra*, and *Whatsaid Serif*. New Directions published the latest installment of "Andoumboulou," *Splay Anthem*, in 2006. Mackey's critical writings are collected in *Discrepant Engagement: Dissonance, Cross-Culturality, and Experimental Writing* and *Paracritical Hinge: Essays, Talks, Notes, Interviews*. He is the founder and editor of *Hambone* magazine; the co-editor of the anthology *Moment's Notice: Jazz in Poetry and Prose*; and the host of a legendary radio show of jazz and world music in Santa Cruz called "Tanganyika Strut."

DUNYA MIKHAIL

An Iraqi born in 1965, Mikhail writes in Arabic, Aramaic, and English. Forced into exile in 1995 by the Saddam Hussein regime because of her antiwar book *Diary of a Wave Outside the Sea*, she now lives in Detroit. In 2001 she received the United Nations Human Rights Award for Freedom of Writing. New Directions published *The War Works Hard* in 2005.

The translator ELIZABETH ANN WINSLOW is a fiction writer. Her translation of *The War Works Hard* is her first book.

MICHAEL PALMER

An American born in New York City in 1943 and long resident in San Francisco, essentially all of Palmer's poetry is published by New Directions: *At Passages* (1995); *The Lion Bridge: Selected Poems 1972–1995* (1998); *The Promises of Glass* (2000); *Codes Appearing:*

Poems 1979–1988 (2001); and *Company of Moths* (2005). He is the translator of works by Emmanuel Hocquard, Vicente Huidobro, and Alexei Parshchikov, among others, and the editor of *Code of Signals: Recent Writings in Poetics.* For over thirty years he has collaborated with the Margaret Jenkins Dance Company.

NICANOR PARRA

A Chilean poet and physicist born in 1914, Parra has taken the precision of scientific language and the plain speech of North American modernism and mixed it with his own sardonic humor to invent what he calls "antipoetry," a poetry pitched against Latin American high rhetoric. New Directions has published *Poems and Antipoems* (1967); *Emergency Poems* (1972); *Antipoems: New and Selected* (1985); and *Antipoems: How to Look Better & Feel Great* (2004). Also in English translation is *Sermons and Homilies of the Christ of Elqui.*

The translator LIZ WERNER worked closely with Parra on the newest volume of *Antipoems,* some of which were taken from the poet's notebooks and unpublished in Spanish. It is her first book.

OCTAVIO PAZ

A Mexican born in 1914, Paz was an immensely prolific poet, translator, literary and visual art critic, historian, magazine editor, anthologist, and political analyst. His complete works in Spanish takes up fifteen very large volumes. In 1946, New Directions published the first translations of Paz in any language. These were followed by *Sun Stone* (translated by Muriel Rukeyser, 1963); *Configurations* (1971); *Early Poems 1935–1955* (1973); the prose poems *Eagle or Sun?* (1976); *A Draft of Shadows and Other Poems* (1979); *Selected Poems* (1984); *The Collected Poems 1957–1987* (1987); *A Tree Within* (1988); *Sunstone* (translated by Eliot Weinberger, 1991); *A Tale of Two Gardens: Poems from India 1952–1995* (1997); and a collaboration with his wife, the artist Marie-José Paz, *Figures & Figurations* (2002). Among his many other books in English translation are: *The Labyrinth of Solitude*; *Sor Juana, or the Traps of Faith*; *Conver-*

gences: Essays on Art and Literature; *The Double Flame: Love and Eroticism*; and *In Light of India*. He received the Nobel Prize in 1990. Octavio Paz died in 1998; "Response and Reconciliation" was his last poem.

JEROME ROTHENBERG

An American born in New York City in 1931, Rothenberg is a poet, anthologist, translator, and energetic general impresario of the perennial avant-garde. His books of poetry from New Directions are: *Poems for the Game of Silence* (1971); *Poland/1931* (1974); *A Seneca Journal* (1978); *Vienna Blood* (1980); *That Dada Strain* (1983); *New Selected Poems 1970–1985* (1986); *Khurbn & Other Poems* (1989); *The Lorca Variations* (1993); *Seedings & Other Poems* (1996); *A Paradise of Poets* (1999); and *A Book of Witnesses: Spells & Gris-Gris* (2003). His essays on poetics are collected in *Pre-Faces & Other Writings* (1981). He is the translator of Schwitters, Nezval, Picasso, Lorca, and Enzensberger, among many others. His anthologies include: *Technicians of the Sacred*; *Shaking the Pumpkin*; *Symposium of the Whole*; *Exiled in the World*; the two-volume *Poems for the Millennium*; and *A Book of the Book*.

AHARON SHABTAI

An Israeli poet born in 1939, Shabtai is notorious for his poems of frank erotic confessionalism and political rage, which appear regularly in the leading newspaper, *Ha'aretz*. On another side, he is the primary translator of classical Greek literature into Hebrew. New Directions published his *J'Accuse* in 2003. Also available in English is *Love & Selected Poems*.

The translator PETER COLE is the author of two books of poetry, *Rift* and *Hymns & Qualms*. His translations of medieval Hebrew poetry include *Selected Poems of Shmuel HaNagid* and *Selected Poems of Solomon Ibn Gabirol*, and a forthcoming general anthology. New Directions published his translations of the contemporary Israeli writer Yoel Hoffmann: *The Heart is Katmandu* (2001) and *The Shunra and the Schmetterling* (2004). He is also the translator from the Arabic of the Palestinian poet Taha Muhammad Ali. He is the co-director of Ibis Editions in Jerusalem.

KAZUKO SHIRAISHI

A Japanese poet born in Vancouver in 1931, Shiraishi's family moved to Japan shortly before the war. As a teenager, she was involved in the surrealist VOU group, and later became known as Japan's leading Beat poet, reading her poems to jazz, and championing artistic, spiritual, and sexual expressions. New Directions published *Seasons of Sacred Lust*, edited by Kenneth Rexroth, in 1975, and *Let Those Who Appear* in 2002; *My Floating Mother, City* is forthcoming.

The translators YUMIKO TSUMURA and the late SAMUEL GROLMES have translated two books by Ryuichi Tamura, as well as the recent collections of Shiraishi.

GUSTAF SOBIN

An American born in Boston in 1935, Sobin moved to the south of France as a young man to study with René Char and Martin Heidegger, and spent the rest of his life there. New Directions published three books of his poetry; *The Earth as Air* (1984); *Voyaging Portraits* (1988); and *Breath's Burials* (1995); and his translation of Henri Michaux's *Ideograms in China* (1984). Other poetry volumes include: *By the Bias of Sound: Selected Poems 1974–1994*; *Toward the Blanched Alphabets*; and *The Places as Preludes*. His novels are *Venus Blue*; *Dark Mirrors: A Novel of Provence*; *The Fly-Truffler*; and *In Pursuit of a Vanishing Star*. He is the author of an extraordinary archeological meditation, *Luminous Debris: Reflecting on Vestige in Provence and Languedoc*; a second volume, *Ladder of Shadows*, is forthcoming. Gustaf Sobin died in 2005.

CHARLES TOMLINSON

An English poet and painter born in 1927, Tomlinson has long lived in Brook Cottage in the Gloucester countryside. His international perspective and particular interest in U.S. poetry is rare for British poets of his generation. A *Collected Poems* appeared in 1985; since then, he has published *The Return*; *Jubilation*; *Anunciations*; *The Door in the Wall*; *The Vineyard Beyond the Sea*; and *Skywriting*. He collaborated with Octavio Paz on the sequences *Hijos del Aire/Airborn* and *Renga*. His books of criticism include *Some Americans*; *Poetry and Metamorphosis*; *American Essays: Making It New*; and *Metamorphoses: Poetry and Translation*. He is the editor of *The Oxford Book of Verse in English Translation*, and books or special issues of magazines devoted to William Carlos Williams, George Oppen, Louis Zukofsky, Marianne Moore, and the Black Mountain poets. Among his many translations are works by Octavio Paz, Antonio Machado, César Vallejo, and Attilio Bertolucci. New Directions published his *Selected Poems 1955–1997* in 1997 and his edition of Williams' *Selected Poems* in 1985.

Tomas Tranströmer

A Swedish poet born in Stockholm in 1931, Tranströmer worked as a psychologist. He has written ten books of short and very short poems; his "epic," *Baltics*, is eight pages; his prose autobiography, *Memories Look at Me*, is 28. New Directions will publish *The Great Enigma: New and Collected Poems* in 2006. The best-known Scandanavian poet of the postwar period, and the most widely translated, his other books available in English include; *Selected Poems 1954–1986*; *The Half-Finished Heaven*; *For the Living and the Dead*; *Night Vision*; and *Windows and Stars*. For many years seriously debilitated by a stroke, Tranströmer continues to write. "The Great Enigma," presented here in its entirety, is his most recent work, completed in 2004.

The translator Robin Fulton is a Scottish poet long resident in Norway. He has translated some thirty books of poetry and prose, most recently works by Henrik Nordbrandt and Olav Hauge. His many books include: *Selected Poems 1963–1978*; *Fields of Focus*; *Coming Down to Earth*; and *The Way the Words Are Taken: Selected Essays*.

Rosmarie Waldrop

An American born in a small town in Bavaria in 1935, Waldrop has written over fifty books of poetry, fiction, critical prose, and translations, as well as collaborations with her husband, Keith Waldrop, with whom she has directed Burning Deck Press for many decades. New Directions has published four books of her poetry: *The Reproduction of Profiles* (1987); *A Key into the Language of America* (1994); *Reluctant Gravities* (1999); and *Blindsight* (2003). Among her other books of poetry is *Another Language: Selected Poetry*. She is the primary working translator of contemporary French and German poetry, including fourteen books by Edmond Jabès (and a remarkable memoir and critical study of Jabès, *Lavish Absence*), and works by Jacques Roubaud, Elke Erb, Oskar Pastior, Emmanuel Hocquard, Paul Celan, and Frederike Mayröcker, among many others.

INDEX

Homero Aridjis

    Self-Portrait at Six Years of Age   95

    A Wounded Self-Portrait   95

    Self-Portrait at Age Ten   98

    Self-Portrait at Eleven on a Train   98

    Self-Portrait at Thirteen Years of Age   99

    Self-Portrait at Age Sixteen   100

    Self-Portrait at Fifty-Four Years Old   101

    Self-Portrait in the Doorway   102

Gennady Aygi

    Again: Air in the Tops – Of Birches   159

    House – In the Grove of the World   160

    Supper: House Outside of Town   161

    House in the Field   162

    Two Epilogues   163

    Fields of this Summer   164

    This August's Phloxes   165

    From Lines in a Dream   166

    Quietness with a Happening   166

    During a Friend's Illness   167

    Day – Towards Evening   167

    Beginning from the Field   168

    The People Are a Temple   168

Bei Dao

    June   59

    Reading   60

    Untitled ("A trumpet . . .")   61

    Leaving Home   62

    Smells   63

    Postwar   63

    Night Sky   64

    Mission   65

In Memory 66

Moon Festival 67

Ramallah 68

The Rose of Time 69

KAMAU BRATHWAITE

The Visibility Trigger 203

How Europe Underdeveloped Africa 206

Stone 213

ANNE CARSON

The Truth About God 46

INGER CHRISTENSEN

from Alphabet 123

ROBERT CREELEY

Edges 226

Life & Death 228

The Way 235

HANS FAVEREY

Eighteen Poems 169

FORREST GANDER

Mission Thief 25

GU CHENG

The Holy Child Descends 35

Crossing the Border 36

Days Gone By 36

from Liquid Mercury 37

The Gaze 44

Oman 45

Seven Days 45

Words 45

SUSAN HOWE

Silence Wager Stories 114

LULJETA LLESHANAKU

Half Past Three 6

Still Life 7

Electrolytes 8
Absence 8
Betrayed 9
Chronic Appendicitis 10
The Awakening of the Eremite 11
Out of Boredom 12
Self-Defense 13

NATHANIEL MACKEY
Song of the Andoumboulou: 46 70
Song of the Andoumboulou: 56 75

DUNYA MIKHAIL
The War Works Hard 14
An Urgent Call 15
America 17
Non-Military Statements 23

MICHAEL PALMER
The Words 83
Construction of the Museum 84
"or anything resembling it" 85
Autobiography 2 (hellogoodby) 86
Una Noche 88
I Do Not 89
Dream of a Language that Speaks 92
The Thought 94

NICANOR PARRA
Seven Voluntary Labors and One Seditious Act 236
Something Like That 237
To Make a Long Story Short 240
A Resounding Zero 240
Note on the Lessons of Antipoetry 241

OCTAVIO PAZ
Response and Reconciliation 1

JEROME ROTHENBERG
At Tsukiji Market Tokyo 179

AHARON SHABTAI
   Nostalgia   103
   Rosh Hashanah   104
   Our Land   105
   Basel Square   107
   Hebrew Culture   108
   Hope   109
   Sharon Resembles a Person   112
   As We Were Marching   113
KAZUKO SHIRAISHI
   A Bear of the Human Family   185
   The Residents of the Cocoon   186
   The Wild Pigs of Kalimantan   187
   From the Precious Tears of the Donkey   188
   The Donkey   Speculates   188
   The Afternoon of the Sheep   189
   The Seven Cats Are Happy   190
GUSTAF SOBIN
   Fourteen Irises for J.L.   137
   Anguish & Metaphor   141
   On the Nature of the Iconic   142
   Sixth Ode: The Grottoes   144
CHARLES TOMLINSON
   Song   218
   Second Song   219
   Zipangu   220
TOMAS TRANSTRÖMER
   The Great Enigma   191
ROSMARIE WALDROP
   from Hölderlin Hybrids   147

Eliot Weinberger

Eliot Weinberger's books of literary essays include *Works on Paper* (NDP 627), *Outside Stories* (NDP 751), and *Karmic Traces* (NDP 908). His political articles are collected in *What Happened Here: Bush Chronicles* (NDP 1020). He is the author of a study of Chinese poetry translation, *19 Ways of Looking at Wang Wei*, and the editor of *American Poetry Since 1950: Innovators & Outsiders* and *The New Directions Anthology of Classical Chinese Poetry* (NDP 1001). His many translations of the work of Octavio Paz include the *Collected Poems 1957–1987* (NDP 719), *In Light of India, Sunstone* (NDP 735), and *A Tale of Two Gardens* (NDP 841). Among his other translations are Vicente Huidobro's *Altazor*, Xavier Villaurrutia's *Nostalgia for Death*, Jorge Luis Borges' *Selected Non-Fictions* and *Seven Nights* (NDP 576), and *Unlock* by Bei Dao (NDP 901).

New Directions Poetry—A Partial Listing

Valentine Ackland, *The Nature of the Moment* (cloth).
John Allman, *Loew's Triboro*. NDP989.
Eugénio de Andrade, *Forbidden Words*.† NDP948.
Guillaume Apollinaire, *Selected Writings*.† NDP310.
Homero Aridjis, *Eyes to See Otherwise*.† NDP942.
Gennady Aygi, *Child-And-Rose*. NDP954.
Jimmy Santiago Baca, *Black Mesa Poems*. NDP676
Martín and Meditations. NDP648.
Immigrants in Our Own Land. NDP701.
Winter Poems Along the Rio Grande. NDP987.
Carol Jane Bangs, *The Bones of the Earth*. NDP563.
Willis Barnstone (trans.), *To Touch the Sky: Poems of Mystical, Spiritual & Metaphysical Light*. NDP900.
Charles Baudelaire, *Flowers of Evil*.† NDP684.
Paris Spleen. NDP294.
Bei Dao, *Midnight's Gate* (essays). NDP1008.
At the Sky's Edge.† NDP934.
Unlock.† NDP901.
Old Snow.† NDP727.
Gottfried Benn, *Primal Vision*.† NDP322.
Johannes Bobrowski, *Shadow Lands: Selected Poems*. NDP788.
Kamau Brathwaite, *Ancestors*. NDP902.
MiddlePassages. NDP776.
Black + Blues. NDP815.
Edwin Brock, *The River and the Train*. NDP478.
William Bronk, *Selected Poems*. NDP816.
Basil Bunting, *Complete Poems*. NDP976.
Hayden Carruth, *Tell Me Again How...* NDP677.
Asphalt Georgics. NDP591
From Snow and Rock, from Chaos. NDP349.
For You. NDP298.
Anne Carson, *Glass, Irony and God*. NDP808.
René Char, *Selected Poems*.† NDP734.
Inger Christensen, *alphabet*. NDP920.
Butterfly Valley. NDP990.
Tom Clark, *Robert Creeley and the Genius...* (w/ Creeley's *Autobiography*, cloth).
Cid Corman, *Nothing/Doing: Selected Poems*. NDP886.
Gregory Corso, *An Accidental Autobiography* (letters). NDP974.
Herald of the Autochthonic Spirit. NDP522.
The Happy Birthday of Death. NDP86.
Robert Creeley, *If I Were Writing This* (cloth).
Life & Death. NDP903.
Echoes (cloth).
Windows (cloth).
H.D., *Analyzing Freud: Letters of H.D., Bryher and Their Circle* (cloth).
Collected Poems. NDP611.
Helen in Egypt. NDP380.
Hermetic Definition. NDP343.
Hippolytus Temporizes & Ion. NDP967.
Selected Poems. NDP658.
Trilogy. NDP866.
Robert Duncan, *Ground Work*. NDP1030.
Bending the Bow. NDP255.
The Opening of the Field. NDP356.
Roots and Branches. NDP275.
Selected Poems. NDP838.
Richard Eberhart, *The Long Reach*. NDP565.

Gavin Ewart, *Selected Poems*. NDP655.
Hans Faverey, *Against the Forgetting*. NDP969.
Lawrence Ferlinghetti, *A Coney Island...* NDP74.
A Far Rockaway of the Heart. NDP871.
How to Pain Sunlight. NDP946.
Americus, Book One. NDP1024.
Thalia Field, *Incarnate: Story Material*. NDP996.
Point and Line. NDP899.
Forrest Gander, *Eye Against Eye*. NDP1026.
Science & Steepleflower. NDP861.
Torn Awake. NDP926.
Goethe, *Faust (Part I)*. NDP70.
Allen Grossman, *Sweet Youth*. NDP947.
How to Do Things with Tears. NDP912.
Gu Cheng, *Sea of Dreams*. NDP1004.
Guillevic, *Selected Poems* (cloth).†
Lars Gustafsson, *Elegies and Other Poems*. NDP898.
Sam Hamill, *The Infinite Moment: Poems from Ancient Greek*. NDP586.
Samuel Hazo, *Thank A Bored Angel*. NDP555.
William Herrick, *That's Life*. NDP596.
David Hinton, *Mountain Home: The Wilderness Poetry of Ancient China*. NDP1009.
Paul Hoover, *The Novel*. NDP706.
Susan Howe, *The Midnight*. NDP956.
The Europe of Trusts. NDP939.
Pierce-Arrow. NDP878.
Frame Structures: Early Poems 1974-1979. NDP822.
The Nonconformist's Memorial. NDP755.
Hsieh Ling-Yün, *The Mountain Poems*. NDP928.
Vicente Huidobro, *The Selected Poetry*.† NDP520.
Philippe Jaccottet, *Seedtime*. NDP428.
Robinson Jeffers, *Cawdor and Medea*. NDP293.
Mary Karr, *The Devil's Tour*. NDP768.
Bob Kaufman, *The Ancient Rain*. NDP514.
Solitudes Crowded with Loneliness. NDP199.
John Keene, *Annotations*. NDP809.
Shimpei Kusano, *Asking Myself/Answering Myself*. NDP566.
Deborah Larsen, *Stitching Porcelain*. NDP710.
James Laughlin, *Byways*. NDP1000.
The Love Poems of James Laughlin. NDP865.
Poems New and Selected. NDP857.
Comte de Lautréamont, *Maldoror*. NDP207.
Irving Layton, *Selected Poems*. NDP431.
Denise Levertov, *Making Peace*. NDP1023.
The Great Unknowing: Last Poems. NDP910.
The Life Around Us. NDP843.
Selected Poems. NDP968.
Poems 1972-1982. NDP913
The Stream and the Sapphire. NDP844.
Li Ch'ing-Chao, *Complete Poems*. NDP492.
Li Po, *The Selected Poems*. NDP823.
Enrique Lihn, *The Dark Room*.† NDP452.
Luljeta Lleshanaku, *Fresco*. NDP941.
Federico García Lorca, *The Cricket Sings*.† NDP506.
Five Plays. NDP506.
In Search of Duende.† NDP858.
Selected Letters. NDP557.
Selected Poems.† NDP1010.
Hugh MacDiarmid, *Selected Poems* (cloth).

For a complete listing request a free catalog from New Directions, 80 Eighth Avenue, New York, NY 10011; or visit our website, www.ndpublishing.com

†Bilingual

Nathaniel Mackey, *Splay Anthem*. NDP112.
Stéphane Mallarmé, *A Tomb for Anatole*. NDP1014.
　Mallarmé in Prose. NDP904.
　Selected Poetry and Prose.† NDP529.
Bernadette Mayer, *Scarlet Tanager*. NDP1015.
　Midwinter Day. NDP876.
　A Bernadette Mayer Reader. NDP739.
Michael McClure, *Rain Mirror*. NDP887.
Thomas Merton, *Collected Poems*. NDP504.
　Gandhi on Non-Violence. NDP197.
　New Seeds of Contemplation. NDP337.
　In the Dark Before Dawn: New Selected Poems.
　NDP1005.
Henri Michaux, *Ideograms in China*. NDP929.
　Selected Writings.† NDP263.
Dunya Mikhail. *The War Works Hard*. NDP1006.
Henry Miller, *The Wisdom of the Heart*. NDP94.
　The Henry Miller Reader. NDP269.
Frédéric Mistral, *The Memoirs*. NDP632.
Eugenio Montale, *Selected Poems*.† NDP193.
　It Depends: A Poet's Notebook (cloth).†
Pablo Neruda, *The Captain's Verses*.† NDP991.
　Residence on Earth,† NDP992.
　Spain in Our Hearts.† NDP1025.
John Frederick Nims, *The Six-Cornered Snowflake*
　(cloth).
Charles Olson, *Selected Writings*. NDP231.
Toby Olson, *Human Nature*. NDP897.
George Oppen, *New Collected Poems* (cloth).
　Selected Poems. NDP970.
Wilfred Owen, *Collected Poems*. NDP210.
José Pacheco, *Battles in the Desert*. NDP637.
Michael Palmer, *The Company of Moths*. NDP1003.
　The Promises of Glass. NDP922.
　Codes Appearing: Poems 1979-1988. NDP914.
　The Lion Bridge: Selected Poems 1972-1995.
　NDP863.
Nicanor Parra, *Antipoems: New and Selected*. NDP603.
Boris Pasternak, *Safe Conduct*. NDP77.
Kenneth Patchen, *Collected Poems*. NDP284.
　Selected Poems. NDP160.
Octavio Paz, *The Collected Poems*.† NDP719.
　Configurations.† 303.
　A Draft of Shadows.† NDP489.
　Figures and Figurations (cloth).†
　Selected Poems. NDP574.
　Sunstone.† NDP735.
　A Tale of Two Gardens: Poems from India. NDP841.
　Eagle or Sun?.† NDP422.
Saint-John Perse, *Selected Poems*.† NDP547.
Po Chü-i, *The Selected Poems*. NDP880.
Ezra Pound, *ABC of Reading*. NDP89.
　The Cantos of Ezra Pound. NDP824.
　Confucius.† NDP285.
　Confucius to Cummings. NDP126.
　A Draft of XXX Cantos. NDP690.
　Personae. NDP697.
　The Pisan Cantos. NDP977.
　The Spirit of Romance. NDP1028.
Mary de Rachewiltz, *Ezra Pound, Father &*
　Teacher. NDP 1029.
Margaret Randall, *Part of the Solution*. NDP350.
Kenneth Rexroth, *Classics Revisited*. NDP621.
　Collected Longer Poems. NDP309.

Collected Shorter Poems. NDP243.
100 Poems from the Chinese. NDP192.
100 Poems from the Japanese. NDP147.
Selected Poems. NDP581.
Rainer Maria Rilke, *Poems from the Book of Hours*.†
　NDP408.
　Possibility of Being, NDP436.
　Where Silence Reigns. NDP464.
Arthur Rimbaud, *Illuminations*.† NDP56.
　A Season in Hell & The Drunken Boat.† NDP97.
Jerome Rothenberg, *A Book of Witness*. NDP955.
　New Selected Poems 1970-1985. NDP625.
　A Paradise of Poets. NDP888.
St. John of the Cross, *The Poems of St. John ...* †
　NDP341.
Jean-Paul Sartre, *Baudelaire*. NDP233.
Delmore Schwartz, *Last and Lost Poems*. NDP673.
　Screeno: Stories and Poems. NDP985.
Peter Dale Scott, *Coming to Jakarta*, NDP672.
　Listening to the Candle. NDP747.
Aharon Shabtai, *J'Accuse*. NDP957.
Kazuko Shiraishi, *Let Those Who Appear*. NDP940.
C.H. Sisson, *Selected Poems*. NDP826.
Stevie Smith, *Collected Poems*. NDP562.
　New Selected Poems. NDP659.
　Some Are More Human Than Others. NDP680.
Gary Snyder, *The Back Country*. NDP249.
　Look Out. NDP949.
　Myths and Texts. NDP457.
　Regarding Wave. NDP306.
　Turtle Island. NDP306.
Gustaf Sobin, *Breaths' Burials*. NDP781.
　The Earth as Air. NDP569.
　Voyaging Portraits. NDP651.
Muriel Spark, *All the Poems of Muriel Spark*. NDP988.
Enid Starkie, *Arthur Rimbaud*. NDP254.
Jules Supervielle, *Selected Writings* (cloth).
Nathaniel Tarn, *Lyrics for the Bride of God*. NDP391.
Dylan Thomas, *The Poems of Dylan Thomas* (cloth,
　w/ CD).
　Selected Poems 1934-1952. NDP958.
Tian Wen: *A Chinese Book of Origins*.† NDP624.
Charles Tomlinson, *Selected Poems*. NDP855.
Tu Fu, *The Selected Poems*, NDP675.
Paul Valéry, *Selected Writings*.† NDP184.
Rosmarie Waldrop, *A Key into the Language of*
　America. NDP798.
　Blindsight. NDP971.
　Reluctant Gravities. NDP889.
　The Reproduction of Profiles (cloth).
Eliot Weinberger, *Karmic Traces*. NDP908.
John Wheelwright, *Collected Poems*. NDP544.
Tennessee Williams, *Collected Poems* (cloth).
William Carlos Williams, *Asphodel ...* NDP794.
　Collected Poems: Volumes I & II. NDP730 &
　NDP731.
　Imaginations. NDP329.
　In the American Grain. NDP53.
　I Wanted to Write a Poem. NDP469.
　Paterson: Revised Edition, NDP806.
　Pictures from Breughel. NDP118.
　Selected Essays. NDP273.
　Selected Poems. NDP602.
　The William Carlos Williams Reader. NDP282.

For a complete listing request a free catalog from New Directions, 80 Eighth Avenue
New York, NY 10011; or visit our website, www.ndpublishing.com

†Bilingual